THE VOYSEY INHERITANCE

HARLEY GRANVILLE-BARKER

Harley Granville-Barker was born in London in 1877. An actor, producer, director, critic, and playwright, he staged important productions of the plays of George Bernard Shaw, and he revolutionized the performance of Shakespeare with his emphasis on naturally spoken dialogue. In addition to *The Voysey Inheritance*, his own plays include *Prunella*, *Waste*, and *The Madras House*. He also wrote a series of five *Prefaces to Shakespeare*, landmark interpretations that consider the plays from the practical perspective of the producer. Granville-Barker died in Paris in 1946.

DAVID MAMET

David Mamet was born in Chicago in 1947. He studied at Goddard College in Vermont and at the Neighborhood Playhouse School of Theater in New York. He has taught at Goddard College, the Yale School of Drama, and New York University, and lectures at the Atlantic Theater Company, of which he is a founding member. He is the author of the plays *The Cryptogram*, *Oleanna*, *Speed-the-Plow*, *Glengarry Glen Ross*, *American Buffalo*, and *Sexual Perversity in Chicago*. He has also written screenplays for such films as *House of Games* and the Oscar-nominated *The Verdict*, as well as *The Spanish Prisoner*, *The Winslow Boy*, and *Wag the Dog*. His plays have won the Pulitzer Prize and the Obie Award.

ALSO BY DAVID MAMET

THE VOYSEY INHERITANCE

❖   ❖   ❖

THE VOYSEY INHERITANCE

❖ ❖ ❖

A Play

HARLEY GRANVILLE-BARKER

Adapted by

DAVID MAMET

VINTAGE BOOKS

A DIVISION OF RANDOM HOUSE, INC.

NEW YORK

A VINTAGE ORIGINAL, OCTOBER 2005

Copyright © 2005 by David Mamet

This work is adapted from *The Voysey Inheritance*
by Harley Granville-Barker, first published in 1905.

Library of Congress Cataloging-in-Publication Data
Mamet, David.
The Voysey inheritance : a play / Harley Granville-Barker ; adapted
by David Mamet.
p. cm.
"A Vintage original"—T.p. verso.
1. Fathers and sons—Drama. 2. Embezzlement—Drama.
I. Granville-Barker, Harley, 1877–1946. Voysey inheritance. II. Title.
PS3563.A4345V695 2005
812'.54—dc22
2005048459

Vintage ISBN-10: 0-307-27519-1
Vintage ISBN-13: 978-0-307-27519-6

www.vintagebooks.com

Printed in the United States of America
10 9 8 7 6 5 4 3 2 1

THE VOYSEY
INHERITANCE

❖   ❖   ❖

PRODUCTION NOTES

The Voysey Inheritance was originally commissioned and produced by American Conservatory Theater, San Francisco (Carey Perloff, Artistic Director; Heather Kitchen, Executive Director) and Kansas City Repertory Theatre (Peter Altman, Producing Artistic Director; William Prenevost, Managing Director). It received its world premiere on March 23, 2005, at the American Conservatory Theater's Geary Theater and opened in Kansas City on April 29, 2005, at the Spencer Theatre, University of Missouri–Kansas City.

MR. VOYSEY	Ken Ruta
MRS. VOYSEY	Barbara Marsh Oliver

Their Children

TRENCHARD VOYSEY	Mark Robbins
HONOR VOYSEY	Cheryl Weaver
MAJOR BOOTH VOYSEY	Andy Murray
EDWARD VOYSEY	Anthony Fusco
HUGH VOYSEY	Stephen Caffrey
ETHEL VOYSEY	Lauren Grace

ALICE MAITLAND	René Augesen
PEACEY	Mark Robbins
MR. GEORGE BOOTH	Gary Neal Johnson
REVEREND EVAN COLPUS	Julian López-Morillas

Director	Carey Perloff
Set Designer	Ralph Funicello
Lighting Designer	Russell H. Champa
Costume Designer	Deborah Dryden
Sound Designer	Garth Hemphill
Casting Director	Meryl Lind Shaw
Dramaturg	Paul Walsh
Production Stage Manager	Mary R. Honour
Assistant Stage Manager	Melissa Cihia Meyer

ONE

❖　❖　❖

Library of the Voysey estate.

EDWARD, *in evening dress, enters the room, followed by* ALICE, *two young people perhaps in their thirties.*

ALICE: You didn't say a word at dinner.

EDWARD: Did I not?

ALICE: A more engagée response might be, "My dear cousin, forgive me . . . business matters," and so on.

EDWARD: I beg your pardon.

ALICE: ... Yes, or, perhaps, "My dear. You've found me out again. The press of work, so on ... banishes e'en the thought of you from my mercantile soul."

EDWARD: Forgive me.

ALICE: Why?

EDWARD: Father's still at the table.

ALICE: And you were late.

EDWARD: I beg your pardon, Alice.

ALICE: Thank you, from which must one not conclude that you are working much too hard; or, if observant, that you have lost all interest in me?

(*Enter* MRS. VOYSEY, *a woman of a certain age.*)

MRS. VOYSEY: He has what, my dear?

ALICE: I say, your son has lost all interest in me.

MRS. VOYSEY: We have lost interest? What is she saying, Edward? Why are you speaking of business; haven't we spoken enough of business?

EDWARD: She isn't speaking of business, Mother.

MRS. VOYSEY: If not, then she will be unique among our family. Edward. I take my oath. Have you seen my "work"?

ALICE: I believe I saw it in the blue room.

MRS. VOYSEY: What?

ALICE: I believe, I saw it in the . . .

MRS. VOYSEY: In the blue room.

(GEORGE BOOTH, *an older gentleman, enters.*)

MRS. VOYSEY: (*Exiting*) What is this interest that they say we've lost?

GEORGE BOOTH: On my word, I've no idea. Edward: is there something I should know?

ALICE: I said he's lost interest in me . . .

GEORGE BOOTH: Oh, good. Then we needn't tighten our belts, eh.

ALICE: That's right.

GEORGE BOOTH: Lost interest in Alice, Edward.

ALICE: Yes, and the shame of it all, after these long years of protestations.

GEORGE BOOTH: You staying up this weekend, Alice, or you going back to town?

ALICE: No, Mr. Booth, I am to stay here, pining, pining . . .

GEORGE BOOTH: Over what? Our, our universal understanding is that it's you have been the long-sought quarry . . . Hugh coming up, Edward?

EDWARD: I beg your pardon.

GEORGE BOOTH: I say: Is Hugh coming up?

EDWARD: I believe he is.

GEORGE BOOTH: I wanted to tell him something. What did I want to tell him?

(MR. VOYSEY, *the paterfamilias, enters.*)

GEORGE BOOTH: Ah, ah, may we, now the cloth is drawn, proceed to business?

MR. VOYSEY: At dinner, George, at dinner?

GEORGE BOOTH: Uh, no, we're on to the port—we're on to the port, eh?

(*Enter* PEACEY, *a middle-aged man in business attire, carrying his overcoat and hat.*)

GEORGE BOOTH: (*Of* PEACEY) And what is this, then?

PEACEY: Evening, Mr. Booth.

GEORGE BOOTH: Good evening, Peacey, what news?

PEACEY: No news, such as is news, Mr. Booth, just these indents to sign . . . (*He passes papers to* MR. VOYSEY, *from the briefcase which he carries.*) And I beg your pardon, to disturb your evening.

GEORGE BOOTH: What of our Australian bonds, Mr. Peacey?

PEACEY: The bonds? Sound as a nut, sir.

GEORGE BOOTH: There's no worry, then? No need for drastic measure, fear of want, and so on. (*Pause*)

MR. VOYSEY: He's joking with you, Peacey.

PEACEY: Well, I know it, sir. (*Noticing* EDWARD) Ah. Mr. Edward. Evening, sir . . . And Miss Alice.

ALICE: Good evening, Peacey . . .

MR. VOYSEY: How's my boy doing, Peacey?

PEACEY: Like his father and his grandfather before him, sir, all business, through and through.

MR. VOYSEY: High praise indeed. (*He finishes with the forms.*)

PEACEY: And in the office, working double tides all weekend.

MR. VOYSEY: In the office on the weekend, was he, Peacey?

PEACEY: Yes, sir.

MR. VOYSEY: Ah ha.

PEACEY: Like father like son, if I may.

MR. VOYSEY: Yes. I understand.

PEACEY: I'm sorry to disturb your evening, sir.

MR. VOYSEY: No, it's good you came. Good you came.

(*The party enters from the dining room.*)

MR. VOYSEY: (*To* PEACEY) Tell Simmons that if he satisfies you on the details of the lease it'll be all right. Make a note for me of Mr. Garinger's address at Mentone, (*Pause*) and I'll take care of the Atkinson letter first thing Monday morning.

PEACEY: Very good, sir.

GEORGE BOOTH: Peacey . . .

MAJOR BOOTH VOYSEY: (*A strapping fellow in middle-age, entering*) Of course I'm hot and strong for conscription.

GEORGE BOOTH: (*To* PEACEY) Nothing urgent, eh? Eh?

MAJOR BOOTH VOYSEY: Get 'em out there, get their knees brown.

GEORGE BOOTH: My dear boy, the country'll never stand for it.

MAJOR BOOTH VOYSEY: If we, if the Army, no, you're quite wrong George, if we lay the hand to the heart, the Army mind you, and say, to the country, on our honor, conscription is essential for your safety.

MR. VOYSEY: Thank you, Peacey . . .

PEACEY: (*Taking his leave*) Sir . . . good evening, gentlemen.

MAJOR BOOTH VOYSEY: Then, what answer, eh?

PEACEY: Miss Alice.

MAJOR BOOTH VOYSEY: What answer has the country? Eh?

MR. VOYSEY: Well, you ask the country.

MAJOR BOOTH VOYSEY: Perhaps I shall, perhaps I shall. Perhaps I'll chuck the service, and go into the House.

(MR. VOYSEY *goes after* PEACEY.)

MR. VOYSEY: Ah, Peacey, the one more thing . . . (*He exits.*)

MAJOR BOOTH VOYSEY: A life of service? I'm not a conceited man, but I believe, were I to speak out, on a subject, which I understand, Edward, eh? Eh?

EDWARD: Mmm?

MAJOR BOOTH VOYSEY: And only on that subject, then, the House will listen. Have to listen.

GEORGE BOOTH: Do you think the gentlemen of England will allow themselves to be herded with a lot of shopkeepers and ploughmen, and be forced to carry guns?

ALICE: Yes, Major, what'd you say to that . . . ?

MAJOR BOOTH VOYSEY: One moment: have you thought, have you thought of the great physical improvement which conscription would bring in the manhood of the country?

GEORGE BOOTH: I thought of it, dear boy, when you brought it up those many—several times during dinner.

MAJOR BOOTH VOYSEY: Yes, but Edward wasn't there, and I'd like his opinion. Where were you, boy, by the way?

ALICE: I believe he has a mistress. (*Pause*)

MAJOR BOOTH VOYSEY: Ah, no, he doesn't have a mistress. You don't have a mistress, do you? Then, where were you, boy?

EDWARD: I was at work.

ALICE: A mistress might be a sign of passion.

MAJOR BOOTH VOYSEY: Quite right. Then, let me ask you, to think, of the moral and physical improvement which conscription would bring in the manhood of this country, Edward . . . S'what this country needs.

ALICE: What is that, Major?

MAJOR BOOTH VOYSEY: Chest. Chest and discipline. These are the fundaments of honor.

(MR. VOYSEY *reenters*.)

MR. VOYSEY: Ah, yes, son, back upon conscription?

MAJOR BOOTH VOYSEY: Edward didn't hear it.

MR. VOYSEY: No, we must all hear it. Mustn't we?

MAJOR BOOTH VOYSEY: You've taught us to speak out, haven't you, sir?

MR. VOYSEY: It seems I have. (*To* COLPUS, *a clerical man, as he enters*) Ah, Vicar . . .

MAJOR BOOTH VOYSEY: By the by, what was Peacey doing here?

MR. VOYSEY: (*To* COLPUS) You were at Lady Mary's t'other evening, weren't you . . . ?

MAJOR BOOTH VOYSEY: Nothing wrong at the shop, eh?

COLPUS: Yes, I was.

MR. VOYSEY: She giving us anything toward our chapel window?

COLPUS: Five pounds more. She's promised me five pounds.

MR. VOYSEY: Then how will the debt stand?

MAJOR BOOTH VOYSEY: . . . Nothin' wrong at the shop . . . ?

GEORGE BOOTH: Oh, please . . .

COLPUS: The debt will be, it will be thirty-three, no, I tell a lie, thirty-five pounds.

MR. VOYSEY: Still . . .

COLPUS: Oh, yes.

MR. VOYSEY: We're a long time, clearing it off.

COLPUS: Well, now that the window's up, people don't seem quite so willing to contribute.

MAJOR BOOTH VOYSEY: We must mention that to Hugh.

COLPUS: Not that Hugh's work ain't universally admired. I have heard Hugh's work praised by the most competent of judges.

MAJOR BOOTH VOYSEY: As it should be.

COLPUS: And Trenchard has subscribed two pounds.

MR. VOYSEY: When is Hugh coming?

GEORGE BOOTH: When is Hugh coming? I saw the window—
that's what I wanted to tell him.

COLPUS: But perhaps . . .

GEORGE BOOTH: . . . And I admired it.

COPLUS: Perhaps it would have been wise to delay the unveiling
until the debt had been cleared.

MR. VOYSEY: Well, it was my wish that my son should do the
design. I suppose, in the end, I'll have to send a check.
What do you say Edward?

GEORGE BOOTH: I saw his design for the window and I thought
it was quite pleasant.

MR. VOYSEY: Edward?

EDWARD: Father?

MR. VOYSEY: Are you sleeping, boy? You didn't eat enough to
get you groggy . . .

GEORGE BOOTH: Perhaps he's in love.

MAJOR BOOTH VOYSEY: He's been in love for years, why should it break out now?

ALICE: Why, indeed.

MAJOR BOOTH VOYSEY: He been neglecting you? Say the word, and I'll take him out and cane him.

ALICE: Thank you, sir.

MAJOR BOOTH VOYSEY: See if I don't. Girl like that. What's wrong with you, boy, you lack "initiative."

(ETHEL, *a beautiful girl in her thirties, enters.*)

ETHEL: Father. You men have been in here too long.

ALICE: Thank you, Ethel.

ETHEL: Oh, you know . . . And Mother asks: have you taken your pill?

(HONOR, *the older sister, follows* ETHEL *into the library.*)

ETHEL: And you're to come back.

HONOR: (*Prompting* ETHEL) "Has he taken his pill?"

ETHEL: And you're to come back.

MR. VOYSEY: And, why, why does she want us back? Honor?

HONOR: It's not Mother wants us back.

MR. VOYSEY: Who is it, then?

HONOR: Ethel wants to convene a free and frank discussion of her wedding present.

ETHEL: That's not true. Well, it is true, but it's not pleasant.

MR. VOYSEY: Why not, darling?

ETHEL: It's not pleasant to be tagged as avaricious, really, Honor.

EDWARD: Really, Honor.

HONOR: Yes, yes . . .

ETHEL: And, in fact, in fact, if you will, I have decided, Dennis and I have decided that we want no wedding present.

EDWARD: What do you want, a check?

ETHEL: That's right. We want a check.

MAJOR BOOTH VOYSEY: Well, that's blunt, that's awfully blunt, innit?

ETHEL: (*To* MR. VOYSEY) We feel a check will give greater scope to your generosity. Of course, if you, in your benevolence, decide to add some "trimmin's," in the shape of a piano, or a turkey carpet, well. But, all in all, Dennis and I would be over the moon for a check.

MR. VOYSEY: You're a minx.

ETHEL: What's the use of having money, if you don't spend it on me?

MR. VOYSEY: What am I going to do with you?

ETHEL: Come to the billiard room, I want to play billiards.

MR. VOYSEY: Now she wants us to play billiards, why?

ETHEL: To display my innate superiority.

MR. VOYSEY: To hear is to obey . . .

(*He rises, and all except* EDWARD *begin to follow him.*)

ETHEL: And Mother asks have you taken your pill.

MR. VOYSEY: I've had my pill.

ETHEL: Scout's honor. Seriously.

MR. VOYSEY: Yes. I have.

ETHEL: Come on, then.

(EDWARD *remains seated.*)

ETHEL: Edward, you, too.

EDWARD: Yes, I'll be right along. Father . . .

GEORGE BOOTH: Eh? And the bonds. What of the Australian bonds?

MR. VOYSEY: No, no business . . .

EDWARD: Father . . .

MR. VOYSEY: No more business tonight . . . And where are my Havanas? Honor?

HONOR: In the billiard room.

MR. VOYSEY: They're in the billiard room, well, then . . .

MAJOR BOOTH VOYSEY: (*Exiting*) You coming, Edward . . . ?

GEORGE BOOTH: Stick with the bonds, eh? Should I stick with the bonds?

MR. VOYSEY: Well, I'll ask *you*: why stick with 'em?

GEORGE BOOTH: The high interest.

MR. VOYSEY: Question, then, what do you want with it, you never spend half your income.

GEORGE BOOTH: Forty-two percent is pleasing.

MR. VOYSEY: That's what it is: you're a buccaneer.

GEORGE BOOTH: As long as I have you to advise me.

MR. VOYSEY: The man who don't know must trust in the man who does.

GEORGE BOOTH: Oh, my Lord, what shall I do when you're gone . . .

MR. VOYSEY: Well, there's Edward . . .

GEORGE BOOTH: Well, Edward, yes . . . (*To* EDWARD) No offense . . . No offense, Edward, I meant no offense.

EDWARD: I'm sure you did not, sir . . .

GEORGE BOOTH: (*To* HONOR) But, he's not his father, is he . . . ? (*He exits.*)

HONOR: Now, he knows the Havanas live in the billiard room. Wherever else would they be?

ALICE: Where, indeed.

HONOR: What a difficult, difficult family, Alice. All except Edward.

EDWARD: Why me?

ALICE: Yes, I shall save the city, should you find me just the one honorable man.

MR. VOYSEY: (*Calling, offstage*) Honor.

HONOR: Yes, Father . . . (*Leading* EDWARD *and* ALICE)

ALICE: (*Pause*) The Pettifers asked after you.

EDWARD: Were they here?

ALICE: Yes. They left early . . .

EDWARD: Ah.

ALICE: I spent August with them, you know. (*Pause*) Did you know that?

EDWARD: Yes, I knew.

ALICE: May I suppose you missed me? (*Pause*) What is it, Edward?

EDWARD: No, it's nothing.

ALICE: You haven't, you haven't even proposed to me, since I've got back.

EDWARD: And?

ALICE: I miss it. My word, how you've become disagreeable.

(MR. VOYSEY *sticks his head back into the library.*)

MR. VOYSEY: Are you coming, Edward?

ALICE: Your son's turned cold, Mr. Voysey.

MR. VOYSEY: Cold toward you? Then that's cold, indeed. What's wrong with the boy?

ALICE: I fear he has found someone else. (*Pause*) And I had so looked forward to his arrival. (*She exits.*)

MR. VOYSEY: (*Pause*) S'all right between you and her, is it? (*Pause*) You should have seen her primping all this afternoon, eh, in respect of your arrival. (*Pause*) Good girl. (*Pause*) Come on, then, join the party.

EDWARD: Father.

MR. VOYSEY: What is it? (*Pause*) What is it? (*He goes to the door and closes it.*) Mmm?

EDWARD: I, uh . . .

MR. VOYSEY: All right, whatever it is. Whatever the mess is: you won't have been the first. And you won't be the first to get clear of it. Now, you tell me: what is it? It's some girl, eh?

EDWARD: Father.

MR. VOYSEY: (*Pause*) It wouldn't be the first time in life. If that's what it is—it can be dealt with, but it must be faced.

(ETHEL *comes into the library.*)

ETHEL: Mother says come now, the both of you, or it'll be the worse for you.

MR. VOYSEY: We'll be right there.

ETHEL: No, I'm to fetch you.

MR. VOYSEY: Thank you, dear, we'll be right along.

ETHEL: Having a heart-to-heart, are we?

MR. VOYSEY: Just a chat.

ETHEL: Don't turn lugubrious, I've told you, now, that you're wanted.

MR. VOYSEY: I've known few things, in my life, couldn't be threshed out in a quarter-hour.

ETHEL: I'm going to hold you to it. (*She exits.*)

MR. VOYSEY: Now: You didn't come down Saturday, you come home tonight, two hours late. Where have you been and what is it?

EDWARD: I've been at the office.

MR. VOYSEY: Then tell me what is the damned gallows look? Whatever it is, we'll work it out.

EDWARD: You've bankrupted the firm. The firm is bankrupt. (*Pause*) What have you done with the money? What have you done with the money?

MR. VOYSEY: Let's begin again, shall we?

EDWARD: I went through all the papers twice. (*He produces a sheaf of papers.*)

MR. VOYSEY: Now, wait wait, when did this begin?

EDWARD: Oh, Father.

MR. VOYSEY: When did this begin?

EDWARD: I've been down there all weekend, I . . . (*Pause*)

MR. VOYSEY: I can't hear you.

EDWARD: I was going through Mrs. Murberry's account. Friday, Friday night . . .

MR. VOYSEY: . . . Why didn't you come to me?

EDWARD: I wanted to make sure.

MR. VOYSEY: Sure of what? . . . Sure of what?

EDWARD: I went through all of them twice, Father.

MR. VOYSEY: Pull yourself together. Do you hear me? Now, it seems you've giv'n yourself a bad forty-eight hours. I wish you had come to me, but let's thresh this thing out now. It's all right. You went through Mrs. Murberry's account.

EDWARD: I . . .

MR. VOYSEY: I can't hear you.

EDWARD: Yes. I did.

MR. VOYSEY: And you found?

EDWARD: Is this a test? Is it a test?

MR. VOYSEY: Of what?

EDWARD: Are you testing me?

(ETHEL *throws open the doors.*)

ETHEL: Are you coming in, or must we send a constable?

MR. VOYSEY: We'll be right in.

ETHEL: Because I'm getting cross.

MR. VOYSEY: We have a little business.

ETHEL: Why can't you leave it at the office? Edward. Have you learned nothing? Truly. Are you a shopkeeper ruining our evening? Sunday evening, Edward. We expected you on Friday night.

MR. VOYSEY: We'll be right in.

ETHEL: Well, I say it's too bad. Sitting in here with a briefcase. (*To* EDWARD) D'you hear me? Why do you act like this? Father's not a well man. He's worked like a slave all week. You've disappointed him, now must you dog him, too? (*Pause*) Must we . . . ? (*Exits*)

MR. VOYSEY: Shall we table this? (*Rises*)

EDWARD: Mrs. Murberry's account is empty. It shows no balance. She has no money in her account.

MR. VOYSEY: We have her money in the bank.

EDWARD: No . . . we've got the lease of her present house, several agreements . . . and here's her will. Here's also a sometime-expired power of attorney, over her securities and her properties generally . . . it was for six months . . .

MR. VOYSEY: She was in South Africa . . .

EDWARD: . . . the power of attorney, now expired, twelve years ago. Here is the Sheffield mortgage.

MR. VOYSEY: Her money's in the bank.

EDWARD: And the Henry Smith mortgage, with banker's receipts . . . hers to us for the interest up to date. Four and a half and five percent. Here's a list of her bonds. And a memorandum in your writing that they are at the bank.

MR. VOYSEY: As I said.

EDWARD: But you neglect to say which bank.

MR. VOYSEY: It's my own . . . Stukeley's . . .

EDWARD: Your own. I marked that with a query. There's eight thousand five hundred in three and a half India stock. And there are her banker's receipts for checks on account of those dividends. I presume for those dividends.

MR. VOYSEY: Of course they are—why not?

EDWARD: (*Gravely*) Because then, Father, there are banker's half yearly receipts amounting to an average of four hundred and twenty pounds a year. But I find no record of any capital to produce this sum. (*Pause*) Till about three years back there seems to have been eleven thousand in Queensland which would produce—did produce exactly the same sum. But after January of that year I find no record of these bonds.

MR. VOYSEY: . . . I must rest.

EDWARD: There is no record of the Queensland bonds.

MR. VOYSEY: In fact, the bonds—you say the bonds are missing.

EDWARD: They are missing.

MR. VOYSEY: From which you conclude?

EDWARD: I concluded at first that you had not handed me all the papers connected with—

MR. VOYSEY: You said there were two cases.

EDWARD: Yes. The Hatherley trust.

MR. VOYSEY: Quite so.

EDWARD: (*With one accusing glance*) Trust.

MR. VOYSEY: Go on.

EDWARD: Oh, Father . . .

MR. VOYSEY: I know, my dear boy. I shall have much to say to you. But let's get quietly through with these details first.

EDWARD: Yes, this is simple enough. We're young Hatherley's only trustees till his coming of age in about five years' time. The property was eighteen thousand invested in Consol's. Certain sums were to be allowed for his education; these have been and are still being paid. There is no record as to the rest of the capital.

MR. VOYSEY: None?

EDWARD: Yes . . . I beg your pardon, sir. There's a memorandum to refer to the Bletchley land scheme.

MR. VOYSEY: That must be ten years ago. But he's credited with the interest on his capital?

EDWARD: On paper, sir. The balance was to be reinvested. There's a partial account in your handwriting. He's credited with the Consol interest.

MR. VOYSEY: Yes?

EDWARD: I think I've heard you say that the Bletchley scheme paid seven and a half.

MR. VOYSEY: At one time. Have you taken the trouble to calculate what will be due from us to the lad?

EDWARD: Capital and compound interest . . . about twenty-six thousand pounds.

MR. VOYSEY: Yes, it's a large sum. In five years' time?

EDWARD: When he comes of age.

MR. VOYSEY: Well, that gives us, say four years and six months in which to consider it. (*Pause*)

EDWARD: I don't understand.

MR. VOYSEY: Don't you?

EDWARD: There are no funds in these accounts. In the accounts we manage. (*Pause*) There are no funds. (*Pause*) How long has it been going on?

MR. VOYSEY: I'm sorry to involve you in it.

EDWARD: Involve me? I'm your partner. I'm responsible too . . . You, we have defrauded everyone who has trusted us. How can you simply sit there? Father. What is the extent of the, the . . . What made you begin it?

MR. VOYSEY: I didn't begin it.

EDWARD: You didn't. Who, then?

MR. VOYSEY: My father before me. (EDWARD *stares.*)

EDWARD: But I . . .

MR. VOYSEY: It's my inheritance.

EDWARD: My dear father?

MR. VOYSEY: I'd hoped it wasn't to be yours.

EDWARD: D'you mean to tell me that this sort of thing has been going on for years? For more than thirty years!

MR. VOYSEY: We do what we must in this world, Edward. I have done what I had to do.

EDWARD: Go on.

MR. VOYSEY: Shall I . . . ? (*Pause*) Yes, I suppose I must. You know that I'm heavily into Northern Electrics.

EDWARD: Yes.

MR. VOYSEY: But you don't know how heavily. When I discovered the municipalities were organizing the purchase, I thought, of course, the stock'd be up a hundred and forty—a hundred and fifty in no time. Now Leeds won't make up their quarrel with the other firm . . . there'll be no bill brought in now for ten years. I bought at ninety-five. What are they now?

EDWARD: Eighty-eight.

MR. VOYSEY: Eighty-seven and a half. (*Pause*)

EDWARD: With whose money are you so heavily into Northern Electrics?

MR. VOYSEY: The firm's.

EDWARD: Clients' money?

MR. VOYSEY: Yes.

EDWARD: . . . I'm waiting for your explanation.

MR. VOYSEY: Children always think the worst of their parents. I did of mine. It's a pity.

EDWARD: Go on, sir. Let me know the worst.

MR. VOYSEY: There's no immediate danger. I should think anyone could see that from the state of these accounts. In truth, there's no actual danger at all.

EDWARD: Is that the worst?

MR. VOYSEY: Have you studied these two accounts, or have you not?

EDWARD: I have, sir.

MR. VOYSEY: Well, here's the deficiency in Mrs. Murberry's income . . . has she ever gone without a shilling? What has young Hatherley lost?

EDWARD: He stands to lose—

MR. VOYSEY: He stands to lose nothing if I'm spared for a time, and you will only bring a little common sense to bear, and try to understand the difficulties of my position.

EDWARD: Father, I'm not thinking ill of you . . . that is, I'm trying not to. But won't you explain how you're justified—?

MR. VOYSEY: In putting our affairs in order?

EDWARD: And are you doing that?

MR. VOYSEY: Your grandfather, Edward, made a grave misjudg-
ment. Then the money went, and what was he to do?
He'd no capital, no credit, and was in terror of his life. My
dear Edward, if I hadn't found it out he'd have confessed
to the first man who came and asked for a balance sheet.

EDWARD: Well, what exact sum was he to the bad then?

MR. VOYSEY: I forget. Several thousands.

EDWARD: But surely it has not taken all these years to pay off—

MR. VOYSEY: Oh, hasn't it!

EDWARD: (*Making his point*) But how does it happen, sir, that
such a comparatively recent trust as a young Hatherley's
has been broken into?

MR. VOYSEY: Well, what could be safer than to use that money?
There's a Consol investment, and not a sight wanted of
either capital or interest for five years.

EDWARD: Father, are you mad?

MR. VOYSEY: My practice is to reinvest my clients' money when
it is entirely under my control. The difference between

the income this money has to bring to them and the income it is actually bringing to me I utilize in my endeavor to fill up the deficit in the firm's accounts . . . in fact, to try and put things straight. Doesn't it follow that the more low-interest-bearing capital I can use, the better . . . the less risky things I have to put it into. Most of young Hatherley's Consol capital is out on mortgage at four and a half and five . . . safe as safe can be.

EDWARD: But he should have the benefit.

MR. VOYSEY: He has the amount of the interest.

EDWARD: Are the mortgages in his name?

MR. VOYSEY: Some of them . . . some of them. That's a technical matter. With regard to Mrs. Murberry . . . those Fretworthy bonds at my bank . . . I've raised five thousand on them. I can release her bonds tomorrow if she wants them.

EDWARD: Where's the five thousand?

MR. VOYSEY: I don't know . . . It was paid into my private account. Yes, I do remember. Some of it went to complete a purchase . . . that and two thousand more out of the Skipworth fund. I . . . Get me a drink, will you?

EDWARD: How, how have you kept it from Peacey?

MR. VOYSEY: Peacey knows—

EDWARD: Peacey knows? Of the theft? Has he always known?

MR. VOYSEY: Of the "theft"?

EDWARD: Yes. It is theft, is it not?

(MR. VOYSEY *considers his son for a moment.*)

MR. VOYSEY: Oh . . . why is it so hard for a man to see beyond the letter of the law. Will you consider a moment, Edward, the position in which I found myself? Was I to see my father ruined and disgraced without lifting a hand to help him? . . . not to mention the interest of the clients. I paid back to the man who would have lost most by my father's mistakes every penny of his money. He never knew the danger he'd been in . . . never passed an uneasy moment about it. It was I who lay awake. I have now somewhere a letter from that man to my father thanking him effusively for the way in which he had conducted business. It comforted my poor father. Well, Edward, I stepped outside the letter of the law to do that. Was that right or wrong?

EDWARD: I cannot say, sir. (*Pause*)

MR. VOYSEY: What would allow you to say? (*Pause*) All right, judge by the result. I took the risk of failure . . . I should have suffered. I could have kept clear of the danger if I'd liked. (*Pause*) Do you see that?

EDWARD: But that's all past. The thing that concerns me is what must we do now.

MR. VOYSEY: But do you see that?

EDWARD: What must we do now?

MR. VOYSEY: My boy, you must trust me. It's all very well for you to come in at the end of the day and criticize. But I, who have done the day's work, know how that work had to be done. And here's our firm, prosperous, respected, and without a stain on its honor. That's the main point, isn't it? And I think that achievement should earn me the right to be trusted a little . . . shouldn't it?

EDWARD: Look here, sir, I'm dismissing from my mind all prejudice about speaking the truth . . . acting upon one's instructions, behaving as any honest firm of solicitors must behave . . .

MR. VOYSEY: You need not. I tell no unnecessary lies. If a man of any business ability gives me definite instructions about his property, I follow them.

EDWARD: Father, please stop.

MR. VOYSEY: Well, my friend, go and tell Mrs. Murberry that four hundred and twenty pounds of her income hasn't for the last eight years come from the place she thinks it's come from, and see if she'd like me to stop.

EDWARD: But is that four hundred and twenty a year as safe to come to her as it was before you meddled with the capital?

MR. VOYSEY: I see no reason why—

EDWARD: What's the security?

MR. VOYSEY: My financial ability.

EDWARD: Do you not realize it's theft?

MR. VOYSEY: Edward, I give all I have to the firm's work . . . my brain . . . my energies . . . my whole life. I can't turn my abilities into hard cash at par . . . I wish I could. Do you suppose that if I could establish every one of these people with a separate and consistent bank balance tomorrow that I shouldn't do it? Do you suppose that it's a pleasure . . . that it's relaxation to have these matters continually on one's mind? Do you suppose—?

EDWARD: I should like you now, sir, if you don't mind, to drop with me all these protestations about putting the firm's affairs straight, and all your anxieties and sacrifices to that end. I see now, of course . . . that for some time, ever since, I suppose, you recovered from the first shock, this hasn't been your object at all. You've used your clients' capital to produce your own income . . . to bring us up and endow us with. Booth's ten thousand pounds; what you are giving Ethel on her marriage . . . my own pocket money as a boy was probably withdrawn from some client's account. You've been very generous to us all, Father. I suppose about half the sum you've spent on us would've put things right.

MR. VOYSEY: No, it would not.

EDWARD: No, there must have been opportunities.

MR. VOYSEY: Must there?

EDWARD: In thirty years? There must have been times.

MR. VOYSEY: Well, if you're so sure, I hope that when I'm gone you may discover them.

EDWARD: I?

MR. VOYSEY: When the burden's yours.

EDWARD: I? God forbid.

MR. VOYSEY: You're my partner, and my son. And you'll inherit the business.

EDWARD: Oh, no, Father . . .

MR. VOYSEY: Why else have I told you?

End of One.

TWO

❖   ❖   ❖

The library, draped in mourning. EDWARD *and* ETHEL.

All characters wear mourning.

GEORGE BOOTH *enters with* MRS. VOYSEY.

GEORGE BOOTH: Edward. (*To* MRS. VOYSEY) Will you come in here?

MRS. VOYSEY: Thank you.

GEORGE BOOTH: I thought it was well done.

MRS. VOYSEY: Yes. (*Pause*) Yes . . .

ETHEL: Will you excuse me . . . ? (ETHEL *exits*.)

(*With great solicitude he puts* MRS. VOYSEY *in a chair; then takes her hand.*)

GEORGE BOOTH: Now I'll intrude no longer.

MRS. VOYSEY: You'll take some lunch?

GEORGE BOOTH: No.

MRS. VOYSEY: Not a glass of wine?

GEORGE BOOTH: If there's anything I can do just send 'round.

MRS. VOYSEY: Thank you.

(*He reaches for the door, only to be met by* MAJOR BOOTH VOYSEY.)

MAJOR BOOTH VOYSEY: I think it all went off as he would have wished.

GEORGE BOOTH: Great credit . . . great credit.

(TRENCHARD VOYSEY *enters.*)

TRENCHARD: Have you the right time?

GEORGE BOOTH: I think so . . . I make it fourteen minutes to one. Trenchard, as a very old and dear friend of your father's, you won't mind me saying how glad I was that you were present today. Death closes all. Indeed . . . it

must be a great regret to you that you did not see him
before . . . before . . .

TRENCHARD: I don't think he asked for me.

GEORGE BOOTH: No? No? Well . . . I . . . I . . .

(HUGH VOYSEY *enters.*)

GEORGE BOOTH: My dear Hugh . . . I won't intrude.

TRENCHARD: Well, Hugh.

HUGH: Yes. Well.

TRENCHARD: Beatrice didn't come down.

HUGH: No . . .

GEORGE BOOTH: . . . Well . . . (*He exits. Pause.*)

MAJOR BOOTH VOYSEY: A glass of wine, Mother. (*Pause*)

MRS. VOYSEY: What?

MAJOR BOOTH VOYSEY: Have a glass of wine?

MRS. VOYSEY: Sherry, please. (*Pause*)

MAJOR BOOTH VOYSEY: No, I thought that was well done. (*Pause*)

MRS. VOYSEY: What?

MAJOR BOOTH VOYSEY: I thought it was well done.

MRS. VOYSEY: Yes.

MAJOR BOOTH VOYSEY: Wine, Edward?

EDWARD: No, thank you.

(ALICE *comes in.*)

ALICE: Edward, Honor has gone to her room. I want to take her some food and make her eat it. She's very upset.

EDWARD: Make her drink a glass of wine, and say it is necessary she should come down here. And d'you mind not coming back yourself, Alice? (*Pause*)

ALICE: Oh. (*Pause*) Certainly, cousin.

MAJOR BOOTH VOYSEY: What's this? What's this?

(ALICE *exits.*)

MAJOR BOOTH VOYSEY: What is this, Edward?

EDWARD: I have something to say to you all.

MAJOR BOOTH VOYSEY: What?

EDWARD: Well, Booth, you'll hear it when I say it.

MAJOR BOOTH VOYSEY: Is it business? . . . Because I think this is scarcely the time for business.

EDWARD: Why?

MAJOR BOOTH VOYSEY: Do you find it easy and reverent to descend on the instant from your natural grief to the consideration of money . . . ? I do not. (*He finds* TRENCHARD *at his elbow.*) I hope you are getting some lunch, Trenchard.

EDWARD: This is business, and more than business, Booth. I choose now, because it is something I wish to say to the family, not write to each individually . . . and it will be difficult to get us all together again.

MAJOR BOOTH VOYSEY: Well, then, as Edward is in the position of trustee . . . as he is executor . . . I don't know your terms . . . I suppose there's nothing more to be said.

TRENCHARD: I don't see what your objection is.

MAJOR BOOTH VOYSEY: Don't you? I should not have called myself a sentimental man, but . . .

HUGH: No. I suppose I'm the sentimental one. I think that's what I am . . .

(HONOR *enters.*)

HONOR: What's wrong with Alice?

MAJOR BOOTH VOYSEY: I say, must we do this now?

EDWARD: Yes. My dear Honor. I am sorry to be so—

HONOR: What is it, please?

MAJOR BOOTH VOYSEY: He's talking business.

HONOR: Now? Now, Edward?

EDWARD: Yes, now.

HONOR: Why have you banished Alice? Is this why? She's weeping on the stairs. You've thrown her out. Why?

EDWARD: Mother? Mother.

MRS. VOYSEY: Yes, Edward?

EDWARD: Mother, we're going to have a little talk. It's over money matters. It is necessary now, because . . . because it's most convenient, and it must be done. Will you sit down? Hugh, would you mind attending?

HUGH: What is it?

EDWARD: There's a chair. (*Pause*)

(HUGH *takes it.*)

MAJOR BOOTH VOYSEY: Well, Edward?

EDWARD: I'll come straight to the point which concerns you. Our father's will gives certain sums to you all . . . the gross amount something over a hundred thousand pounds. There will be no money.

MRS. VOYSEY: I didn't hear. (*Pause*)

HUGH: (*In his mother's ear*) Edward says there's no money.

TRENCHARD: I think you said . . . "will be."

MAJOR BOOTH VOYSEY: Why will there be no money?

EDWARD: Because every penny by right belongs to those clients whom our father spent his life in defrauding. When I say defrauding, I mean it in its worst sense . . . swindling . . . thieving. I have been in the swim of it for the past year endeavoring to . . . and I mean to collect every penny I can; put the firm into bankruptcy; and reimburse these people what we can. I'll stand my trial . . . it'll come to that with me . . . and as soon as possible. (*Pause*) Are none of you going to speak? Quite right, what is there to be said! I'm sorry to hurt you, Mother.

MRS. VOYSEY: I can't hear quite all you say, but I guess what it is. You don't hurt me, Edward . . . I have known of this for a long time.

EDWARD: Oh, Mother, did he know you knew?

MRS. VOYSEY: What do you say?

TRENCHARD: I may as well tell you, Edward, I suspected everything wasn't right about the time of my last quarrel with
my father. Of course, I took care not to pursue my suspi-
cions. Was Father aware that you knew, Mother?

MRS. VOYSEY: We never discussed it. There was once a great
danger . . . when you were all younger . . . of his being
found out. But we never discussed it.

EDWARD: I'm glad it isn't such a shock to you all.

HUGH: My God . . . before the earth has settled on his grave!

EDWARD: I thought it wrong to postpone telling you.

HONOR: Oh, poor papa! . . . Poor papa!

EDWARD: Honor, we shall want your help and advice.

MAJOR BOOTH VOYSEY: I have said nothing as yet, Edward, I am
thinking.

TRENCHARD: That's the worst of these family practices . . . a lot
of money knocking around and no audit ever required.
The wonder to me is to find an honest solicitor at all.

MAJOR BOOTH VOYSEY: Really, Trenchard!

TRENCHARD: Well, the more able a man is the less the word "honesty" bothers him . . . and Father was an able man.

EDWARD: I thought that a year ago.

TRENCHARD: Yes . . .

EDWARD: I thought that at the worst he was a gifted criminal.

MAJOR BOOTH VOYSEY: Really . . . really, Edward!

EDWARD: And everything was to come right in the end . . . we were all to be in reality as wealthy and as prosperous as we have seemed to be all these years. But when he fell ill . . . towards the last . . . the facts came out.

TRENCHARD: And these facts are?

EDWARD: Laughable. You wouldn't believe there were such fools in the world as some of these wretched clients have been. The firm's funds were just a lucky bag into which he dipped. Now sometimes their money doesn't even exist.

MAJOR BOOTH VOYSEY: Where's it gone?

EDWARD: You've been living on it.

MAJOR BOOTH VOYSEY: Good God!

TRENCHARD: What can you pay in the pound?

EDWARD: Without help? . . . six or seven shillings, I daresay. But we must do better than that.

(*To which there is no response.*)

MAJOR BOOTH VOYSEY: All this is very dreadful. Does it mean beggary for the whole family?

EDWARD: It should.

TRENCHARD: Nonsense!

EDWARD: What right have we to a thing we possess?

TRENCHARD: He didn't make you an allowance, Booth . . . your capital's your own, isn't it?

MAJOR BOOTH VOYSEY: Really . . . I . . . I suppose so.

TRENCHARD: Then you're all right.

EDWARD: It's stolen money.

TRENCHARD: I didn't know that.

MAJOR BOOTH VOYSEY: I should hope not.

EDWARD: It's stolen money.

MAJOR BOOTH VOYSEY: I say, what ought I to do?

TRENCHARD: Do . . . my dear Booth? Nothing.

EDWARD: Trenchard, we owe reparation—

TRENCHARD: To whom? From which account was Booth's money taken?

EDWARD: I don't know . . . I daresay from none directly.

TRENCHARD: Very well, then.

EDWARD: You argue as he did—

TRENCHARD: Nonsense, my dear Edward. The law will take anything it has a right to, and all it can get; you needn't be afraid. There's no obligation, legal or moral, for us to throw our pounds into the wreck, that they may become pence.

EDWARD: I can hear my father . . .

TRENCHARD: But what about your own position . . . can we get you clear?

EDWARD: That doesn't matter.

MAJOR BOOTH VOYSEY: But I say, you know, this is awful! Will this have to be made public?

TRENCHARD: What help is there for it?

MRS. VOYSEY: What is all this?

TRENCHARD: Edward wishes us to completely beggar ourselves in order to pay back to every client to whom Father owed a pound perhaps ten shillings instead of seven.

MRS. VOYSEY: He will find that my estate has been kept quite separate.

TRENCHARD: I'm very glad to hear it, Mother.

MRS. VOYSEY: (*Pause*) When Mr. Barnes died, your father agreed to appointing another trustee. I think I'll go to my room. I can't hear what any of you are saying. Edward, you will tell me afterwards.

EDWARD: Would you like to go, too, Honor?

HONOR: Yes, please, I would.

(*They exit.*)

TRENCHARD: How long have things been wrong?

EDWARD: He told me the trouble began in his father's time, and that he'd been battling with it ever since.

TRENCHARD: And is that possible?

EDWARD: Yes. I believed him. Now I look through his papers, I can find only one irregularity that's more than ten years old, and that's only to do with old George Booth's business.

MAJOR BOOTH VOYSEY: But Father never touched his money . . . why, he was a personal friend.

TRENCHARD: Very curious his evolving that fiction about his father . . . I wonder why. I remember the old man. He was as honest as the day.

EDWARD: To gain sympathy, I suppose.

TRENCHARD: What position did you take upon the matter when he told you?

EDWARD: You know what he was as well as I.

TRENCHARD: Well . . . what did you attempt to do?

EDWARD: I urged him to start by making some of the smaller accounts right. He said . . . he said that would be penny-wise and pound-foolish. So I did what I could myself.

TRENCHARD: With your own money?

EDWARD: The little I had.

TRENCHARD: Can you prove that you did that?

EDWARD: I suppose I could.

TRENCHARD: It's a good point.

MAJOR BOOTH VOYSEY: Yes, I must say—

TRENCHARD: You ought to have written him a letter, and left the firm the moment you found out. Even then, legally . . . ! But as he was your father. What was his object in telling you?

EDWARD: I thought, at the time, it was remorse.

TRENCHARD: And now?

EDWARD: Now I really believe it was that he might have someone to boast to of his financial exploits.

TRENCHARD: I daresay.

MAJOR BOOTH VOYSEY: Scarcely matters to boast of.

TRENCHARD: No? You try playing the fool with other people's money, and keeping your neck out of the noose for twelve years. Quite a performance.

EDWARD: Then, of course, he always protested that things would come right . . . that he'd clear the firm and have a fortune to the good. Or that if he were not spared I might do it. But he must have known that was impossible.

TRENCHARD: But there's the gambler all over. "It'll all come right."

EDWARD: Why, he actually took the trouble to draw up this will!

TRENCHARD: That was childish.

EDWARD: And I'm the sole executor.

TRENCHARD: So I should think . . . was I down for anything?

EDWARD: No.

TRENCHARD: How he did hate me!

EDWARD: You're safe from the results of his affection, anyway.

TRENCHARD: What on earth made you stay in the firm, once you knew?

EDWARD: Inertia.

TRENCHARD: No, tell me truly. (*Pause*)

EDWARD: I thought I might prevent things from getting any worse. I think I did . . . well, I should have done that if he'd lived.

TRENCHARD: You knew the risk you were running?

EDWARD: Yes. (*Pause*)

TRENCHARD: I must be off. Business waiting . . . close-of-play, you know.

MAJOR BOOTH VOYSEY: Shall I walk to the station with you?

TRENCHARD: I'll spend a few minutes with Mother. You'll count on my professional assistance, please, Edward.

EDWARD: (*Simply*) Thank you, Trenchard.

(TRENCHARD *goes.*)

HUGH: The more I think this out, the more devilishly humorous it gets. Old Booth breaking down by the grave . . . Colpus intoning the service . . .

EDWARD: Yes, the vicar will be badly hit.

HUGH: Oh, yes, Father managed his business for years.

MAJOR BOOTH VOYSEY: Good God . . . how shall we ever look old Booth in the face again?

EDWARD: I don't worry about him. He can die quite comfortably enough on six shillings in the pound. It's the smaller fry who'll suffer.

MAJOR BOOTH VOYSEY: Now, just explain to me . . . I didn't interrupt while Trenchard was talking . . . of what exactly did this defrauding consist?

EDWARD: Speculating with a client's capital . . . pocketing the gains, cutting the losses; meanwhile paying the client his ordinary income.

MAJOR BOOTH VOYSEY: So the client's kept in the dark.

EDWARD: Quite so.

MAJOR BOOTH VOYSEY: In point of fact, then, the client doesn't suffer?

EDWARD: He doesn't suffer till he finds out.

MAJOR BOOTH VOYSEY: And all that's wrong now is that some of their capital is missing.

EDWARD: Yes, that's all that's wrong.

MAJOR BOOTH VOYSEY: What is the ah . . . deficit?

EDWARD: Anything between two and three hundred thousand pounds.

MAJOR BOOTH VOYSEY: Dear me . . .

HUGH: . . . Quite apart from the rights and wrongs of this, only a very able man could have kept a straight face to the world all these years, as Father did.

MAJOR BOOTH VOYSEY: I suppose he sometimes made money by these speculations.

EDWARD: Very often. His own expenditure was heavy, as you know.

MAJOR BOOTH VOYSEY: He was a generous man.

HUGH: I, I thought that I was the artist. But it would seem it was *he*.

MAJOR BOOTH VOYSEY: That's uncalled for, Hugh.

HUGH: Oh? *Edward.*

EDWARD: Yes.

HUGH: Did no one ever suspect him?

EDWARD: When there was any danger . . . when a trust had to be wound up . . . he'd make the great effort, and put the accounts straight.

MAJOR BOOTH VOYSEY: Then he did put some accounts straight?

EDWARD: Yes, when he couldn't help himself.

HUGH: (*To himself*) . . . Yes. It seems he was the artist . . .

MAJOR BOOTH VOYSEY: Be quiet. Now look here, Edward. You told us that he told you that it was the object of his life to put these accounts in order. Then you laughed at that. Now you tell me that he *did* put some accounts right.

EDWARD: My dear Booth, you don't understand.

MAJOR BOOTH VOYSEY: Well, let me understand. I am anxious to understand.

EDWARD: We can't pay ten shillings in the pound.

MAJOR BOOTH VOYSEY: That's very dreadful. But do you know that there wasn't a time when we couldn't have paid five? (*Pause*)

EDWARD: I don't know.

MAJOR BOOTH VOYSEY: Very well, then! If what he said was true about his father and all that . . . and why shouldn't we believe him if we can? . . . and if he *did* effect an improvement, that's all to his credit. Let us at least be just, Edward.

EDWARD: I am very sorry to appear unjust. He has left me in a rather unfortunate position.

MAJOR BOOTH VOYSEY: Yes, his death was a tragedy. It seems to me that if he had been spared he might have succeeded at length in this tremendous task, and restored to us our family honor.

EDWARD: Yes, Booth, he spoke very feelingly of that.

MAJOR BOOTH VOYSEY: I can well believe it. And I can tell you that now . . . I may be right or I may be wrong . . . I am feeling far less concerned about the clients' money than I am at the terrible blow to the family which this exposure will strike. Money, after all, can to a certain extent be done without . . . but honor—

EDWARD: Our honor! Does one of you mean to give me a single penny towards undoing all the wrong that has been done?

MAJOR BOOTH VOYSEY: I take Trenchard's word for it that that would be illegal.

EDWARD: Well, then, don't talk to me of honor.

MAJOR BOOTH VOYSEY: I am speaking of public exposure. Edward, can't that be prevented?

EDWARD: How?

MAJOR BOOTH VOYSEY: Well . . . how was it being prevented before he died—before we knew anything about it? . . . Do you see? (*Pause*) I am beginning to think that you have worked yourself into rather an hysterical state over this unhappy business.

EDWARD: Perhaps you'd have been glad . . . glad if I'd held my tongue and gone on lying and cheating . . . and married and begotten a son to go on lying and cheating after me . . . and to pay your interest . . . your interest in the crime.

MAJOR BOOTH VOYSEY: Look here, Edward, this rhetoric is exceedingly out of place. The simple question before us is . . . What is the best course to pursue?

EDWARD: There is no question before us. There's only one course to pursue.

MAJOR BOOTH VOYSEY: That is not so. Let me speak, please. Insofar as our poor father was dishonest to his clients, I pray that he may be forgiven. Insofar as he spent his life honestly endeavoring to right a wrong which he had found already committed . . . I forgive him. And I admire him, Edward. And I feel it my duty to—er—reprobate most strongly the—er—gusto with which you have been holding him up in memory to us . . . ten minutes after we have stood around his grave . . . as a monster of wickedness. I think I may say I knew him as well as you . . . better. And . . . thank God! . . . there was not between him and me this—this unhappy business to warp my judgment of him. Did you ever know a more charitable man . . . a larger-hearted? He was a faithful husband . . . and what a father to all of us, putting us out into the world and fully intending to leave us comfortably settled there. Further . . . as I see this matter, Edward . . . when as a young man he was told this terrible secret, and entrusted with such a frightful task . . . did he turn his back on it like a coward? No. He went through it heroically to the end of his life. And as he died I imagine there was no more torturing thought than that he had left his work unfinished. And now if all these clients can be kept receiving their natural income, and if Father's plan could be carried out of gradually replacing the capital—

EDWARD: You're appealing to me to carry on this crime?

MAJOR BOOTH VOYSEY: Haven't you been doing so? (*Pause*) This last year? Since he told you?

EDWARD: Why do you press me?

MAJOR BOOTH VOYSEY: I press you to come to a reasonable position.

EDWARD: Do you want your legacy? Is that it? Shall that count as "reasonable"?

MAJOR BOOTH VOYSEY: In one moment, Edward, I shall become angry. Here I am doing my best to help you, and your clients, and you sit there imputing to me the most sordid motives. Do you suppose I should touch or allow to be touched the money which Father has left us, before every client's claim was satisfied?

EDWARD: My dear Booth, I'm sure you mean well, but . . .

MAJOR BOOTH VOYSEY: And I'll come down to your office and work with you there. I'll help you.

EDWARD: My dear Booth.

MAJOR BOOTH VOYSEY: I, I, I'm not sure what can be done, but whatever can be done, I will be there to help you.

TRENCHARD: (*Offstage*) Are you coming Booth?

MAJOR BOOTH VOYSEY: Yes, I am. (*To* EDWARD) You do nothing rash. I've no doubt we can devise something which will obviate, Edward, which will obviate the necessity . . . and then I'm sure I shall convince you. (*Exits with* TRENCHARD.)

EDWARD: It's strange the number of people who believe you can do right by means which they know to be wrong.

HUGH: Let's say legal and illegal. You're so down on the Governor because he has trespassed against the etiquette of your own profession. But now he's dead . . . and if there weren't the disgrace to think of . . . it's no use the rest of us pretending to feel him a criminal, because we don't. Edward??

EDWARD: Yes?

HUGH: "Don't do anything rash."

(ALICE *enters quietly*.)

EDWARD: How are you, Hugh?

HUGH: I'm as you see me. (*At this point he becomes conscious that* ALICE *is standing behind him*.) Hullo, Alice.

ALICE: Hullo, Hugh. (*Pause*)

HUGH: D'you want to speak to Edward?

ALICE: Please, Hugh.

HUGH: I'll go. (*Exits*.)

ALICE: They have told me.

EDWARD: He was fond of you.

ALICE: Your father.

EDWARD: Mmm.

ALICE: Yes. He was.

EDWARD: Don't think worse of him than you can help.

ALICE: I'm not thinking of him.

EDWARD: No?

ALICE: I'm thinking of you.

EDWARD: I may just escape.

ALICE: So Trenchard says.

EDWARD: My hands are clean, Alice.

ALICE: I know that. (*Pause*)

EDWARD: Mother's not very upset.

ALICE: She had expected the smash in his lifetime, it seems.

EDWARD: I'm glad that didn't happen.

ALICE: Yes . . . as the fault was his it won't hurt you so much to stand up to the blame. (*Pause*) Do you know it was a mercy to tell Honor just at this time. She can grieve for his death and his disgrace at the same time . . . and the one grief lessens the other perhaps.

EDWARD: Oh, they're all shocked enough at the disgrace . . . but will they open their purses to mitigate it?

ALICE: Will it seem less disgraceful to have stolen ten thousand pounds than twenty?

EDWARD: I should think so.

ALICE: I should think so, too—but I wonder if that's the law. If it isn't, Trenchard wouldn't consider the point. I'm sure public opinion doesn't say so . . . and that's what Booth is considering.

EDWARD: Yes. He would.

ALICE: Well, he's in the army . . . he's almost in society . . . and he has to get on in both; one mustn't blame him. Of course, if the money could have been given up with a flourish of trumpets . . . ! But even then I doubt whether the advertisement would bring in what it cost.

EDWARD: But when one thinks how the money was obtained!

ALICE: . . . When one thinks how the money is obtained . . .

EDWARD: They've not earned it.

ALICE: If they had, they might have given it you and earned more. Did I ever tell you what my guardian said to me when I came of age?

EDWARD: I'm thankful your money's not been in danger.

ALICE: It might have been, but I was made to look after it myself . . . much against my will. My guardian was a person of great character and no principles, the best and most lovable man I've ever met . . . I'm sorry you never knew him, Edward . . . and he said once to me . . . You've no right to your money. You've not earned it or deserved it in any way. Therefore, don't be surprised or annoyed if any enterprising person tries to get it from you. He has at least as much right to it as you have. If he can use it better, he has more right. Shocking sentiments, aren't they? No respectable man of business could own to them. (*Pause*) I'm not so sorry for some of these clients as you are, Edward.

EDWARD: You surprise me, Alice.

ALICE: I'm pleased that I still have that capacity. (*Pause*)

EDWARD: . . . One or two of the clients will be beggared.

ALICE: Yes, that is serious. What's to be done?

EDWARD: There's old Nurse . . . with her poor little savings gone!

ALICE: Surely those can be spared her?

EDWARD: The law's no respecter of persons . . . that's its boast. Old Booth, with more than he wants, will keep enough. My old nurse, with just enough, may starve. But it'll be a relief to clear out this nest of lies, even though one suffers oneself. I've been ashamed to walk into that office, Alice . . . I'll hold my head high in prison, though.

ALICE: Edward, I'm afraid you're feeling heroic.

EDWARD: I? Heroic?

ALICE: Don't be so proud of your misfortune. You looked quite like Booth for the moment. It will be very stupid to send you to prison, and you must do your best to keep out. We were discussing if anything could be done for these one or two people who'll be beggared.

EDWARD: Yes, Alice. I'm sorry nothing can be done for them.

ALICE: It's a pity.

EDWARD: I suppose I was feeling heroic. I didn't mean to.

ALICE: That's the worst of acting on principle . . . one begins thinking of one's attitude instead of the import of one's actions.

EDWARD: I'm exposing this fraud on principle.

ALICE: Are you?

EDWARD: Yes—indeed. I am.

ALICE: Perhaps that's what's wrong.

EDWARD: Wrong?

ALICE: My dear Edward, if people are to be ruined . . .

EDWARD: But what else is there to be done?

ALICE: Well . . . have you thought?

EDWARD: There's nothing else to be done.

ALICE: On principle? No? Nothing? (*Pause*)

EDWARD: It had occurred to Booth . . .

ALICE: Oh, anything may occur to Booth.

EDWARD: . . . in his grave concern for the family honor that I might quietly cheat the firm back into credit again.

ALICE: How stupid of Booth.

EDWARD: Well . . . like my father . . . Booth believes in the sanctity of the status quo.

ALICE: Does he indeed?

EDWARD: But don't think I've any talents that way, principles or no. What have I done so far? Sat in the shame of it for a year. I did take a hand . . . if you knew what it felt like . . . I managed to stop one affair going from bad to worse.

ALICE: If that was the best you could do wasn't it worth doing?

EDWARD: And that may cost me . . . at the best I'll be struck off . . . one's livelihood gone.

ALICE: The cost is of course your own affair.

EDWARD: (*Pause*) My affair alone?

ALICE: Is it not?

EDWARD: (*Interrupting*) . . . I'll tell you what I *could* do.

ALICE: Yes?

EDWARD: It's just as irregular.

ALICE: That doesn't shock me . . . I'm lawless by birthright, being a woman.

EDWARD: There are four or five accounts I believe I could get quite square. Mrs. Travers . . . well, she'd never starve, but I'd like to see those young Lyndhursts safe. There's money to play with, Heaven knows. It'd take a while to get it right and cover the tracks. Cover the tracks . . . sounds well, doesn't it?

ALICE: And then you'd give yourself up as you'd meant to do now?

EDWARD: Yes.

ALICE: And?

EDWARD: Go bankrupt.

ALICE: It'd be worse for you at the trial.

EDWARD: You said that was my affair.

ALICE: Oh, Edward!

EDWARD: Shall I do it?

ALICE: Why must you ask me?

EDWARD: Do you know what I like about you, Alice?

ALICE: Yes. I think I do.

End of Two.

THREE

❖   ❖   ❖

The library. The signs of mourning are gone. Some Christmas deco-
rations are to be found. EDWARD, *dressed in traveling clothes, is put-*
ting some papers into a briefcase. PEACEY *enters.*

PEACEY: Good morning, sir.

EDWARD: Good morning, Peacey, good of you to come in on
the holiday.

PEACEY: Well, sir, the work must be done . . .

(EDWARD *holds out his hand and* PEACEY *puts some papers into it.*)

PEACEY: And of course, I always did it, in your father's day, sir.

EDWARD: (*Examining the papers*) I'm sorry, what? You always did what in my father's day?

PEACEY: Whatever needed to be done.

EDWARD: Of course.

PEACEY: And I've arranged your travel, sir.

EDWARD: Yes, thank you. Please see that a dozen roses are sent to my mother—New Year's Day. Here's the card.

PEACEY: Very good, sir.

EDWARD: If Bullen calls, over the holiday, he shouldn't but, in the event, I'll deal with him on the second. Write to Metcalf. Tell him I interviewed Vickery myself, on Friday. Let me see that letter again. (PEACEY *hands* EDWARD *a letter* EDWARD *has just signed and handed him.*) Yes, that's fine. (EDWARD *hands the letter back.*)

PEACEY: Very good, sir.

EDWARD: That will be all. (*Pause*)

PEACEY: May I speak to you a moment, sir?

EDWARD: Can't it wait till I return?

PEACEY: Just a moment, if I may.

EDWARD: Very well. Very well, certainly. (*Pause*) . . .Yes?

PEACEY: Bills are beginning to come in upon me as is usual at this season, sir. My son's allowance at Cambridge is now rather a heavy item of my expenditure. I hope that the custom of the firm isn't to be neglected now that you are the head of it, Mr. Edward. Two hundred your father always made it at Christmas . . . in notes, if you please.

EDWARD: In notes. To be sure . . . your hush money.

PEACEY: That's not a very pleasant word, sir.

EDWARD: This is not a pleasant subject.

PEACEY: I'm sure it isn't my wish to bring out in cold conversation what I know of the firm's position. (*Pause*) Your father always gave me notes in an envelope when he shook hands with me at Christmas.

EDWARD: Yes, I, I rather knew.

PEACEY: You did, sir . . . ?

EDWARD: And I've been waiting for you to ask me.

PEACEY: Well, then, we'll say no more about it. There's always a bit of friction in coming to an understanding about anything, isn't there, sir?

EDWARD: Why didn't you speak to me about this last Christmas?

PEACEY: I knew you were upset at your father's death.

EDWARD: Father died the August before that.

PEACEY: Well . . . truthfully, Mr. Edward?

EDWARD: As truthfully as you think suitable.

PEACEY: Well, I couldn't make you out last Christmas. I'd always thought there must be a smash when your father died . . . but it didn't come. But then again last Christmas you seemed all on edge, and I didn't know what might happen. So I thought I'd better keep quiet and say nothing.

EDWARD: I see. This little pull of yours over the firm is an inheritance from *your* father, isn't it?

PEACEY: When he retired, sir, he said to me . . . "I've told the Governor you know what I know." And Mr. Voysey said to me . . . "I treat you as I did your father, Peacey." I never had another word on the subject with him.

EDWARD: A very decent arrangement. Your son's at Cambridge, you say, Peacey?

PEACEY: Yes.

EDWARD: I wonder you didn't bring him into the firm.

PEACEY: Thank you, sir . . . I thought of it. But then I thought that two generations in this sort of thing was enough.

EDWARD: A fine point of taste.

PEACEY: And then, sir . . . I don't want to hurt your feelings, but things simply cannot go on forever. The marvel to me is that the game has been kept up as it has. So now, if he does well at Cambridge, I hope he'll go to the bar. He has a distinct talent for patiently applying himself to the details of a thing.

EDWARD: Well, then, I'm sure he'll do well. I'm glad to have had this talk with you, Peacey. I'm sorry you can't have the money you want.

PEACEY: Oh, no, any time will do, sir.

EDWARD: You can't have the money at all.

PEACEY: Can't I?

EDWARD: Since my father's death the trust business of the firm has not been conducted as formerly. We no longer make illicit profits out of our clients. There are none for you to share.

PEACEY: Look here, Mr. Edward, I'm sorry I began this discussion. You'll give me my two hundred as usual, please, and we'll drop the subject.

EDWARD: By all means drop the subject.

PEACEY: I want the money. I think it is not gentlemanly in you, Mr. Edward, to make these excuses to try to get out of paying it me. Your father would never have made such an excuse.

EDWARD: Do you think I'm lying to you?

PEACEY: I don't wish to criticize your statements or your actions at all, sir. It was no concern of mine how your father treated his clients.

EDWARD: Indeed.

PEACEY: Indeed, sir—I am an *employee*. I was paid to execute your father's wishes—as a *clerk*, sir—his professional . . .

EDWARD: . . . manipulations?

PEACEY: Were beyond me and were no concern of mine.

EDWARD: Nicely put. And now it's no concern of yours how honest *I* am.

PEACEY: Well, don't be sarcastic . . . a man does get used to a state of affairs whatever it may be, as you have, sir, if I may, as *your* family has, these many years.

EDWARD: My friend, in one moment I shall have to tell you very candidly what I think of you.

PEACEY: That I'm a thief because I've taken money from a thief?

EDWARD: You're worse than a thief. You're content that others should steal for you.

PEACEY: As who isn't? (*Pause*)

EDWARD: Ah, Peacey, I perceive that you study sociology. Well, that's too big a question to enter into now. The application of the present portion of it is that I have for the moment, at some inconvenience to myself, ceased to receive stolen goods and therefore am in a position to throw a stone at you. I have thrown it.

PEACEY: And now I'm to leave the firm, I suppose?

EDWARD: Not unless you wish.

PEACEY: I happen to think the secret's worth its price.

EDWARD: Perhaps someone will pay it you.

PEACEY: You're presuming upon its not being worth my while to make use of what I know.

EDWARD: My good Peacey, it happens to be the truth I told you just now. How on earth do you suppose you can successfully blackmail a man, who has so much to gain by exposure and so little to lose?

PEACEY: I don't want to ruin you, sir, and I have a great regard for the firm . . . but you must see that I can't have my income reduced in this way without objection.

EDWARD: Peacey . . . Peacey. I have, as I believe you're aware, struggled, to return the firm to what you will forgive me if I characterize as a "moral footing." You are not unaware of these efforts. I am near succeeding, as, again, you know. You see all of our incomes reduced. And yet you come to me. Why?

PEACEY: For one thing, sir, I don't think it fair dealing on your part to dock the money suddenly. I have been counting on it most of the year, and I have been led into heavy expenses. Now, couldn't you have warned me?

EDWARD: That's true, Peacey, it was stupid of me. I apologize for the mistake.

PEACEY: Perhaps things may be easier for you by next Christmas.

EDWARD: I hope so.

PEACEY: Then . . . perhaps you won't be so particular.

EDWARD: So you don't believe what I told you?

PEACEY: Yes, I do.

EDWARD: Then you think that the fascination of bilking one's clients will ultimately prove irresistible?

PEACEY: It's what happened to your father. (*Pause*)

EDWARD: Go on.

PEACEY: He got things right as rain once, Mr. Edward. I should be very glad to know that the firm was solvent and going straight. There have been times when I have sincerely regretted my connection with it. If you'll let me say so, I think it's very noble of you to have undertaken the work you have. And Mr. Edward, if you'll give me enough to cover this year's expense I think I may promise you that I shan't expect money again. (*Pause*)

EDWARD: No.

PEACEY: You hesitated, sir.

EDWARD: Then call me a hypocrite. But I am not a thief.

PEACEY: Well, sir, you make things very difficult for me.

EDWARD: As long as you're here, here's a letter from Mr. Cartright which you might attend to. If he wants an appointment with me, don't make one till the New Year. His case can't come on before February.

PEACEY: I am aware of your plans, for your vacation.

EDWARD: I don't understand.

PEACEY: And, I am anxious to meet you in every way—(*Pause*)

EDWARD: (*Holding a file*) "Perceval Building Estate" . . . You may file that, too.

PEACEY: . . . but I refuse to be ignored. I must consider my whole position. I hope I may not be tempted to make use of the power I possess. But if I am driven to proceed to extremities . . .

EDWARD: My dear Peacey, don't talk nonsense . . . you couldn't proceed to an extremity to save your life. You've taken this money irresponsibly for all these years. You'll find you're no longer capable of concerted moral action. (*Pause*)

PEACEY: Is that what you think, of me, sir? (*Pause*) Which would induce you to descend to personalities?

EDWARD: I'm sorry, Peacey.

PEACEY: Is that what you think, that if it happens at the club, it's business, but, backstairs it's theft?

EDWARD: I said I'm sorry.

PEACEY: Yes, sir, yes, indeed you did, as you go off on vacation. And what is paying, if I may, sir, for your fine vacation?

Mr. Voysey? And for your servants? And for the food you eat? Sir?

(HUGH *enters.*)

HUGH: Good morning, Peacey.

PEACEY: I'll take your answer, sir, another day.

EDWARD: That will be all.

PEACEY: Good morning, Mr. Hugh. Good morning, Mr. Edward.

EDWARD: Peacey.

(PEACEY *exits.*)

(HUGH *looks out the window.* EDWARD *finishes packing his briefcase.*)

EDWARD: What brings you down?

HUGH: Eh?

EDWARD: What'd you want?

HUGH: I want a maxim gun planted in Regent Street . . . and one in the Haymarket . . . and one in Leicester Square and one in the Strand . . . and a dozen in the city. An earthquake would be simpler. Or a nice clean tidal wave?

It's no good preaching and patching up any longer, Edward. We must begin, afresh. Don't you feel, even in your calmer moments, that this whole country is simply hideous? The other nations must look after themselves. I'm patriotic . . . I only ask that we should be destroyed.

EDWARD: Perhaps it shall come about.

HUGH: I'm sick of waiting. (*Then as* EDWARD *says nothing*) You say this is the cry of the weak man in despair! I wouldn't be anything but a weak man in this world. I wouldn't be a king, I wouldn't be rich . . . I wouldn't be a Borough Councillor . . . I should be so ashamed. I've walked here this morning from Hampstead. I started to curse because the streets were dirty. You'd think that an empire could keep its streets clean! But then I saw that the children were dirty, too.

EDWARD: That's because of the streets.

HUGH: Yes, it's holiday time. Those that can cross a road safely are doing some work now . . . earning some money. You'd think a governing race, professing responsibilities, might care for its children.

EDWARD: Come, we educate them now. And I don't think many work in holiday time.

HUGH: (*Encouraged by contradiction*) We teach them all that we're not ashamed of . . . and much that we ought to be . . . and the rest they find out for themselves. Oh, every man and woman I met was muddy-eyed! They'd joined the great conspiracy which we call our civilization. They've been educated! They believe in the laws and the money market. (*Pause*) Well, at least they suffer for their beliefs. But I'm glad I don't make the laws . . . and that I haven't any money . . . and that I hate respectability . . . or I should be so ashamed. By the by, that's what I've come for.

EDWARD: What? I thought you'd come to see me off.

HUGH: You must take that money of mine for your clients. Of course you ought to have had it when you asked for it. It has never belonged to me. Well . . . it has never done me any good. I have never made any use of it, and so it has been just a drag on my life.

EDWARD: My dear Hugh . . . this is very generous of you.

HUGH: Not a bit. I only want to start fresh and free.

EDWARD: Hugh, do you really think that money has carried a curse with it?

HUGH: I know it. I'm the proof of it, look at me. When I announced I'd be an artist the Governor gave me a hundred and fifty a year . . . the rent of a studio and the price of a velvet coat he thought it; that was all he knew about art. Then my respectable training got me engaged and married. Marriage in a studio puzzled the Governor, so he guessed it at two hundred and fifty a year . . . What had I to do with art? Nothing I've done yet but reflects our drawing room.

EDWARD: What does your art earn in a year? I doubt if you can afford to give this up.

HUGH: Oh Edward . . . you clank the chain with the best of them. That word "afford"! I want to be free from my advantages. Don't you see I must find out what I'm worth in myself . . . whether I even exist or not? Perhaps I'm only a pretense of a man animated by an income.

EDWARD: But you can't return to nature on the London pavements.

HUGH: No. Nor in England at all . . . it's nothing but a big back garden. (*Pause*) But if there's no place on earth where a man can prove his right to live by some other means than robbing his neighbor . . . I'd better go and request the next horse I meet to ride me . . . to the nearest lunatic asylum.

EDWARD: And what does Beatrice say to your emigrating to the backwoods . . . if that is exactly what you mean?

HUGH: We're separating—

EDWARD: What?

HUGH: We mean to separate.

EDWARD: This is the first I've heard of it.

HUGH: Beatrice is making some money by her books, so it has become possible.

EDWARD: Have you told anyone yet?

HUGH: We mean to now. I think a thing comes to pass quicker in public. (*Pause*) Good this other scandal, eh? Don't you think, Edward . . . ?

EDWARD: Say nothing at home, would you, until after Christmas?

HUGH: Yes, you're right.

EDWARD: I shan't accept this money from you . . . there's no need. All the good has been done that I wanted to do. No one will be beggared now. So why should you be?

HUGH: I was beggared before. Take the blasted money. It ain't mine. It never was.

EDWARD: Consider.

HUGH: I have—anything past this is just cowardice—(*Pause*) Take it. (*Pause*) And you—when will you be quit of the beastly business?

EDWARD: I'm in no hurry.

HUGH: What do you gain by hanging on now?

EDWARD: Occupation.

HUGH: But, Edward, it must be an awfully wearying state of things. I suppose any moment a policeman may knock at the door . . . so to speak?

EDWARD: Any moment. I take no precautions. I suppose that's why he doesn't come. At first I listened for him, day by day. Then I said to myself . . . next week. But a year has gone by and more. I've ceased expecting to hear the knock at all. I've . . . I've decided that "decision" is the thing, and I've decided to get on with my life.

HUGH: But look here . . . is all this worthwhile?

EDWARD: My dear Hugh, what a question!

HUGH: Why should your real happiness be sacrificed to the sham happiness which I believe is called "money"—which people have invested in the firm?

EDWARD: I suppose their money means such happiness to them as they understand.

HUGH: Then we want another currency. I never believed that money was valuable. I once gave a crossing sweeper a sovereign. The sovereign was nothing. But the sensation I gave him was to me a valuable thing.

EDWARD: He could buy other sensations with the sovereign.

HUGH: But none as great as mine. So, yes, we're slaves! Beatrice won't let me go until we're each certain of two hundred a year. And she's quite right . . . I should only go into debt. You know that two fifty a year of mine is a hundred and eighty now.

EDWARD: A hundred eighty, but secure. Finally secure. Thank God. (*Pause*) And made it right. Nearly right.

HUGH: What?

EDWARD: I got it to come nearly right. You needn't give it up. I've nearly balanced the books.

HUGH: But: that is my question, Edward, that is my question.

EDWARD: N'your question is?

HUGH: Is it right? Should we have any of it? (*Pause*)

EDWARD: It says, "The poor are always with us . . ."

HUGH: Yes, but does it follow that the world must bear with the rich?

EDWARD: I'm getting it clear. I've near put it right, God willing I will put it right, and put questions of rich and poor, wrong and right behind me, and let us "be cautioned," and go live a decent life.

(GEORGE BOOTH *enters.*)

GEORGE BOOTH: Hello, Hugh. Hello Edward, I'm glad that I've caught you.

EDWARD: Good morning, Mr. Booth.

HUGH: Well . . . Beatrice and I go down to town tomorrow. I say . . . d'you know that old Nursie is furious with you about something?

EDWARD: Yes, I know. Good-bye.

HUGH: Good-bye. (*Exits.*)

EDWARD: Will you come here . . . or will you sit by the fire?

GEORGE BOOTH: This'll do. I shan't detain you long.

EDWARD: Are you feeling all right now?

GEORGE BOOTH: A bit dyspeptic. How are you?

EDWARD: Quite well, thanks.

GEORGE BOOTH: I'm glad . . . I'm glad. (*Pause*) I'm afraid this isn't very pleasant business I've come upon.

EDWARD: D'you want to go to law with anyone?

GEORGE BOOTH: No . . . oh, no. I'm getting too old to quarrel.

EDWARD: A pleasant symptom.

GEORGE BOOTH: I mean to withdraw my securities from the custody of your firm . . . with the usual notice, of course.

EDWARD: . . . May one ask why?

GEORGE BOOTH: Certainly . . . certainly. My reason is straightforward and simple and well considered. (*Pause*) I think you must know, Edward, I have never been able to feel that implicit confidence in your ability which I had in your father's. Well, it is hardly to be expected, is it? (*Pause*)

EDWARD: No.

GEORGE BOOTH: I can say that without unduly depreciating you. Men like your father are few and far between. As far as I know, things proceed at this office as they have always done, but . . . since his death I have not been happy about my affairs.

EDWARD: I think you need be under no apprehension . . .

GEORGE BOOTH: I daresay not. But that isn't the point. Now, for the first time in my long life, I am worried about money affairs; and I don't enjoy the feeling. The possession of money has always been a pleasure to me . . . and for what are perhaps my last years I don't wish that to be otherwise. You must remember you have practically my entire property unreservedly in your control.

EDWARD: Perhaps we can arrange to hand you over the reins to an extent which will ease your mind, and at the same time not . . .

GEORGE BOOTH: I thought of that. Believe me, I have every wish not to slight unduly your father's son. I have not moved in the matter for eighteen months. I have not been able to make up my mind to. Really, one feels a little helpless . . . and the transaction of business requires more energy than . . . But I saw my doctor yesterday, Edward, and he told me . . . well, it was a warning. And so I felt it my duty at once to . . . especially as I made up my mind to it some time ago. In point of fact, Edward, more than a year before your father died I had quite decided that my affairs could never be with you as they were with him.

EDWARD: Did he know that?

GEORGE BOOTH: I think I never said it in so many words. But he may easily have guessed. (*Pause*)

EDWARD: . . . I hope you won't do this, Mr. Booth.

GEORGE BOOTH: I have quite made up my mind.

EDWARD: You must let me persuade you—

GEORGE BOOTH: I shall make a point of informing your family that you are in no way to blame in the matter. And in the event of any personal legal difficulties I shall always be delighted to come to you. My idea is for the future to employ merely a financial agent—

EDWARD: If you had made up your mind before my father died to do this, you ought to have told him.

GEORGE BOOTH: Please allow me to know my own business best. I did not choose to distress him.

EDWARD: Mr. Booth . . .

GEORGE BOOTH: You're making a fearful fuss about a very simple matter, Edward. The loss of one client, however important he may be . . . Why, this is one of the best family practices in London. I am surprised at your lack of dignity.

EDWARD: Yes. Yes. Should you like a statement now, of your position.

GEORGE BOOTH: Is it necessary? I'll have the papers sent for, after the New Year.

EDWARD: No, I should like to explain some matters to you.

GEORGE BOOTH: And can you do that, absent the documents?

EDWARD: I believe I can.

GEORGE BOOTH: Then, if it's important to you.

EDWARD: Yes, Mr. Booth.

GEORGE BOOTH: Go ahead.

EDWARD: How much do you think you're worth?

GEORGE BOOTH: I couldn't say offhand.

EDWARD: But you've a rough idea?

GEORGE BOOTH: To be sure.

EDWARD: You'll get not quite half that out of us.

GEORGE BOOTH: I think I said I had made up my mind to withdraw the whole amount.

EDWARD: You should have made up your mind sooner.

GEORGE BOOTH: I don't in the least understand you, Edward.

EDWARD: A great part of your capital doesn't exist.

GEORGE BOOTH: You mean that it won't be prudent to realize? You can hand over the securities. I don't want to reinvest simply because—

EDWARD: I can't hand over what I haven't got.

GEORGE BOOTH: Is anything . . . wrong?

EDWARD: We have robbed you of nearly half your property.

GEORGE BOOTH: Say that again.

EDWARD: It's quite true.

GEORGE BOOTH: My money . . . gone?

EDWARD: Yes.

GEORGE BOOTH: You've been the thief . . . you . . . you . . . ?

EDWARD: No.

GEORGE BOOTH: Who, then?

EDWARD: My father.

GEORGE BOOTH: How dare you say that?

EDWARD: It's true.

GEORGE BOOTH: Slandering your dead father . . . and lying to me, revenging yourself by frightening me . . . because I've insulted you.

EDWARD: I . . .

GEORGE BOOTH: *Prove* this . . . prove it to me! I'm not to be frightened so easily. One can't lose half of all one has and then be told of it in two minutes . . .

EDWARD: If my father had told you this in plain words you'd have believed him.

GEORGE BOOTH: Yes. (*Pause*)

EDWARD: Oh, and I was so close. What on earth did you want to withdraw your account for? You need never have known . . . you could have died happy. Settling with all those charities in your will would certainly have smashed us up. But proving your will is many years off yet, we'll hope.

GEORGE BOOTH: I don't understand. No, I don't understand . . . because your father . . . But I must understand, Edward.

EDWARD: Don't shock yourself trying to understand my father, for you never will. Pull yourself together, Mr. Booth. After all, this isn't a vital matter to you. It's not even as if you had a family to consider . . . like some of the others.

GEORGE BOOTH: What others?

EDWARD: Don't imagine your money has been specially selected for pilfering.

GEORGE BOOTH: You mean, you mean *all* of the accounts have been looted? (*Pause*) One has read of this sort of thing, but . . . I thought people always got found out.

EDWARD: Well . . . we are found out. You've found us out.

GEORGE BOOTH: Oh . . . I've been foully cheated!

EDWARD: That's correct.

GEORGE BOOTH: But by you, Edward . . . say it's by you.

EDWARD: I've neither the ability nor the personality for such work, Mr. Booth . . . nothing but principles, which forbid me to lie to you.

GEORGE BOOTH: I think your father is in Hell . . . I'd have gone there myself to save him from it. I loved him very truly. How he could have had the heart! We were friends for nearly fifty years. Am I to think now he only cared for me to cheat me? (*Pause*)

EDWARD: Well, you're master of the situation now. What do you intend to do?

GEORGE BOOTH: To get my money back.

EDWARD: No, that's gone.

GEORGE BOOTH: Then give me what's left, and—

EDWARD: Are you going to prosecute?

GEORGE BOOTH: Oh, dear . . . is that necessary? Can't somebody else do that? I thought the law—

EDWARD: You need not prosecute, you know.

GEORGE BOOTH: What'll happen if I don't?

EDWARD: What do you suppose I'm doing here now?

GEORGE BOOTH: I don't know.

EDWARD: I'm trying to straighten things. I'm trying to undo what my father did . . . to do again what he undid. It's a poor, dull sort of work now . . . throwing penny after slaved-for penny into the pit of our deficit. But I've been doing that for what it's worth, in the time that was left to me . . . till this should happen. I can continue to do that, if you choose . . . until the next smash comes. I'm pleased to call this my duty. It can't hurt you to believe it.

GEORGE BOOTH: You must admit, Edward, it isn't easy to believe anything. Just for the moment.

EDWARD: I can prove it to you. I'll take you through the books . . . you won't understand them . . . but I could prove it.

GEORGE BOOTH: I think I'd rather not. D'you think I ought to hold any further communication with you at all?

EDWARD: Certainly not. Prosecute. Prosecute!

GEORGE BOOTH: Don't lose your temper. You know it's my place to be angry with you.

EDWARD: I beg your pardon. (*Pause*) I shall be grateful if you'll prosecute.

GEORGE BOOTH: There's something in this I don't understand.

EDWARD: Think it over.

GEORGE BOOTH: But surely I oughtn't to have to make up my mind! There must be a right or wrong thing to do. Edward, can't you tell me?

EDWARD: I'm prejudiced.

GEORGE BOOTH: What do you mean by placing me in a dilemma? I believe you're simply trying to practice upon my goodness of heart. Certainly I ought to prosecute at once . . . oughtn't I? Can't I consult another solicitor?

EDWARD: Write to *The Times* about it.

GEORGE BOOTH: Edward, how can you be so cool and heartless?

EDWARD: To you?

GEORGE BOOTH: Yes, to me, Edward. To me. If I have the power to save you. To me. You hard man. Edward: are you your father's son?

EDWARD: Indeed I am.

End of Three.

FOUR

❖   ❖   ❖

The library, now fully decorated for Christmas. ALICE *and* HONOR, *in evening dresses, are arranging little gift baskets.*

HONOR: This is for Mrs. Vickery.

ALICE: Did we remember to include the comforter for the boy?

HONOR: Yes, we did. And you have Mrs. Saunders, over there?

ALICE: I do.

HONOR: I'm glad that Edward stayed on the extra day.

ALICE: Well, I'm sure I am, too.

HONOR: Why is he going off?

ALICE: The pressure of work, I believe, is his foul excuse.

HONOR: Well, I'm glad he stayed. And I'm glad *you* could join us.

ALICE: You don't mind the last-minute acceptance?

HONOR: Do you have my scissors?

ALICE: I believe I do.

(*She passes the scissors.*)

HONOR: The yellow ribbon, please.

ALICE: I believe Ethel has it.

HONOR: Well, she oughtn't to take what is not rightly hers.

(EDWARD *enters in a dinner jacket.*)

HONOR: Do you not agree, Edward?

EDWARD: Good evening, Honor, Alice.

HONOR: And we were just saying how very glad we are you had decided to stay.

ALICE: How very glad, indeed.

HONOR: For, why you'd need to rest, from work, yes, yes, but, from your family?

(ETHEL *enters.*)

HONOR: V'you got my yellow ribbon?

ETHEL: I was wrapping baskets.

HONOR: Quite, but you said you'd give it right back.

ETHEL: I thought I had returned it. Hello, Edward. I wanted to talk to you.

EDWARD: About?

ETHEL: I'd rather not do it here.

EDWARD: About the marriage settlement, again?

ETHEL: I'd rather not do it here.

(HUGH *enters.*)

ETHEL: And what has your wife been telling me?

HUGH: Am I her keeper?

ETHEL: Legally, and morally, yes, I believe, that is the . . .

HONOR: What has she been telling you?

ETHEL: . . . conventional understanding of the marriage contract.

HUGH: And what has she been telling you?

ETHEL: That you mean to separate.

(MAJOR BOOTH VOYSEY *enters.*)

MAJOR BOOTH VOYSEY: (*To* HUGH) There you are. Get your wife.

HUGH: I beg your pardon.

MAJOR BOOTH VOYSEY: What is this we hear?

HUGH: Must you shout?

MAJOR BOOTH VOYSEY: I use the voice nature has gifted me with.

HUGH: And did she not gift you with discretion?

MAJOR BOOTH VOYSEY: This is a family matter, else I should not feel it my duty to interfere. And any member of the family is free to express an opinion. (MRS. VOYSEY *enters.*) Mother:

MRS. VOYSEY: Yes?

HUGH: No one was to be told until after Christmas.

MRS. VOYSEY: What? Told what?

MAJOR BOOTH VOYSEY: Beatrice and Hugh are separating.

MRS. VOYSEY: Separating.

MAJOR BOOTH VOYSEY: And I want to know why.

HUGH: Look here, Booth . . . I will not have you interfering with my private affairs. Is one never to be free from your bullying?

MAJOR BOOTH VOYSEY: You ought to be grateful.

HUGH: Well, I'm not.

MAJOR BOOTH VOYSEY: This is a family affair.

HUGH: It is not!

MAJOR BOOTH VOYSEY: If all you can do is contradict me, you'd better listen to what I've got to say . . . quietly.

ALICE: I believe I should go . . .

(*She moves toward the door, but* MAJOR BOOTH VOYSEY, *standing in the door, does not acknowledge her.*)

MAJOR BOOTH VOYSEY: Why do you wish to separate?

HUGH: We do not get on well together.

ALICE: (*Starting to leave the room*) May I pass, please?

MAJOR BOOTH VOYSEY: Have you thought what this does to the family? To the family, Hugh.

ALICE: May I . . .

MAJOR BOOTH VOYSEY: Please. In words of one syllable.

ALICE: As a maiden lady, Booth, perhaps I might be ex . . .

MAJOR BOOTH VOYSEY: Please. Sit down. Now, why?

HUGH: You don't understand.

MAJOR BOOTH VOYSEY: Well, I surely won't unless you explain yourself.

ETHEL: She's crying upstairs, your wife.

ALICE: (*Pushing past*) You must excuse me. (*She exits.*)

ETHEL: Your wife is crying. Why?

HUGH: She wants more money. (*Pause*) Alpha and omega.

ETHEL: She wants more money.

HUGH: She is angry with me, because I won't dilute my art for money.

MAJOR BOOTH VOYSEY: "Dilute your art" . . .

ETHEL: Why shouldn't she have more money?

HUGH: *I* don't want it.

MAJOR BOOTH VOYSEY: You don't want it. You don't want it. What about your wife?

EDWARD: Might you leave him alone?

MRS. VOYSEY: (*Exiting*) I must say it's beyond me . . . Honor . . . ?

HONOR: (*Rising, and accompanying her*) Yes, Mother. (*Pause*)

MAJOR BOOTH VOYSEY: (*Pause*) You know, I never considered art a very good profession for you, Hugh. And you don't even stick to one department of it. Couldn't you take up something else? In your "spare time"?

EDWARD: Leave him alone.

ETHEL: . . . And while there are folks who want to marry . . .

EDWARD: What's stopping you?

ETHEL: You know very well what's stopping me is money.

EDWARD: Money.

ETHEL: . . . is my marriage settlement, is . . . Yes, as if you ever thought about anything else. Anything else, Edward.

EDWARD: Is that so?

ETHEL: Do you know what you've done, Edward? You've taken yourself out of the family.

HUGH: I wish I might be able to.

ETHEL: It's as if, since Father died, you are become another person.

EDWARD: What person is that, Ethel?

ETHEL: Secretive, standoffish, removed from, from our life, from convention, nothing appeals to you but work; it's wrong, it's underbred, and you may keep your knowing smile, and if this family isn't quite the thing for you, why don't you get out of it . . . ? (*She exits.*)

HUGH: The happy English home.

MAJOR BOOTH VOYSEY: That's enough, I think. That's quite enough. (*Exits.*)

HUGH: What would I not give to escape from it?

(GEORGE BOOTH *enters.*)

HUGH: Good evening.

GEORGE BOOTH: Good evening. Hugh. Edward.

EDWARD: Good evening.

HUGH: We missed you at dinner, sir.

GEORGE BOOTH: Yes, I . . .

EDWARD: Would you excuse us, Hugh?

HUGH: I would. Good evening, sir. (*He exits.*)

EDWARD: Well?

GEORGE BOOTH: I hope my excuse for not coming to dinner was acceptable. I did have . . . I have a very bad headache.

EDWARD: I daresay they accepted it.

GEORGE BOOTH: I have come immediately to tell you of my decision . . . perhaps this trouble will then be a little more off my mind.

EDWARD: What is it?

GEORGE BOOTH: I couldn't think the matter out alone. I went this afternoon to talk it all over with my old friend Colpus. What a terrible shock to him!

EDWARD: Oh, nearly three of his four thousand pounds are quite safe.

GEORGE BOOTH: That you and your father . . . you, whom he baptized . . . should have robbed him! I never saw a man so utterly prostrate with grief. That it should have been your father! And his poor wife! . . . Though she never got on with your father.

EDWARD: Oh, Mrs. Colpus knows, too, does she? The "keeper of the neighborhood's secrets" . . . ?

GEORGE BOOTH: Of course he told Mrs. Colpus. This is an unfortunate time for the storm to break on him. What with Christmas Day and Sunday following so close, they're as busy as can be. He has resolved that during this season of peace and goodwill he must put the matter from him if he can. But once Christmas is over . . .

EDWARD: So I conclude you mean to prosecute. For if you don't, you've given the Colpuses a lot of unnecessary pain . . . and inflicted a certain amount of loss by telling them.

GEORGE BOOTH: I never thought of that. No, Edward, I have decided not to prosecute. I think I could not bear to see the family I have loved brought to such disgrace.

EDWARD: So you'll compound my felony?

GEORGE BOOTH: And I want to ask your pardon, Edward, for some of the hard thoughts I have had of you. I consider this effort of yours to restore to the firm the credit which your father lost a very striking one. What improvements have you effected so far?

EDWARD: With the money that my father left . . .

GEORGE BOOTH: . . . and I suppose you take the ordinary profits of the firm?

EDWARD: A fraction of them. It costs me very little to live.

GEORGE BOOTH: And, let me ask you, do you restore to the clients all 'round, in proportion to the amount they have lost?

EDWARD: That's the law. (*Pause*)

GEORGE BOOTH: D'you think that's quite fair?

EDWARD: No, I don't.

GEORGE BOOTH: No, I consider the treachery to have been blacker in some cases than in others.

EDWARD: As do I.

GEORGE BOOTH: Yes, I am glad to hear it, and this is my proposal. Considering how absolutely I trusted your father, and believed in him, I think you should at once return me the balance of my capital, whatever balance there is, which remains.

EDWARD: That is being done.

GEORGE BOOTH: Good. I suggest that you should continue to pay me a fair interest upon the rest of that capital, which ought to exist and does not. And that you should, year by year, pay me back by degrees out of the earnings of the firm as much of that capital as you can afford. We will agree upon the sum . . . say a thousand a year. I doubt if you can ever restore me all that I have lost, but do your best, and I shan't complain. There . . . I think that is fair dealing.

EDWARD: Fair dealing.

GEORGE BOOTH: It may be more, I don't ask you to thank me. (*Pause*)

EDWARD: How funny! How very funny!

GEORGE BOOTH: Edward.

EDWARD: I never heard anything quite so funny!

GEORGE BOOTH: Edward . . .

EDWARD: What will Colpus . . . what will all the other Christian gentlemen demand? Pounds of flesh?

GEORGE BOOTH: Don't be hysterical. I demand but what is mine . . . in such quantities as you can afford.

EDWARD: I'm giving my soul and body to restoring you and the rest of you to your precious money bags . . . and you'll wring me dry. Won't you? Won't you?

GEORGE BOOTH: Now, be reasonable.

EDWARD: You'd impoverish the smaller investors, in return for your silence.

GEORGE BOOTH: How dare you put it that way?

EDWARD: What other way is there to put it?

GEORGE BOOTH: I demand what is mine.

EDWARD: I DIDN'T TAKE IT. I. Did. Not. Take. It. I am trying to restore it, to you, and to those who were similarly defrauded.

GEORGE BOOTH: AND I AM TRYING TO HELP YOU.

EDWARD: At the price that we pay you first.

GEORGE BOOTH: What world do you suppose you live on?

EDWARD: I . . .

GEORGE BOOTH: Tell me that, boy. Tell me that. With your principles.

EDWARD: What do you know of my principles?

GEORGE BOOTH: Your father would never have acted in this way.

EDWARD: My father was a thief.

GEORGE BOOTH: And what are you? What are you, boy? Living, still, as we do all, as have we, from the profits.

(ALICE *enters, with* COLPUS, *in the midst of* GEORGE BOOTH'*s speech.*)

ALICE: . . . I beg your pardon.

EDWARD: Mr. Colpus . . .

COLPUS: . . . Did you tell him our offer . . . ?

GEORGE BOOTH: What in the world do you think you are? To pass judgment on us, who trusted you . . .

ALICE: I must go.

COLPUS: George Booth has told me of his offer. On his behalf, and on mine . . . on mine. I urge you Edward, and, should you like, I will addend precedent, for accepting our . . .

EDWARD: "Precedent"?

COLPUS: For accepting his kind offer. (*Pause*) Yes.

EDWARD: "Precedent." Do you mean "scripture"?

ALICE: Excuse me . . .

GEORGE BOOTH: No, stay, stay, for I want you to hear this . . .

EDWARD: . . . Can you mean "*scripture*"?

COLPUS: Scripture, yes, scripture, yes. George Booth, George Booth has offered you the chance to make amends, to those who have been wronged by your malfeasance.

EDWARD: My malfeasance . . . ?

COLPUS: And I *quote* you scripture, Edward—and I quote you: "Do not side with the rich against the powerless neither . . ."

EDWARD: (*Starting to exit*) . . . excuse me.

COLPUS: "Neither, *neither* fault the poor, but do *justice* . . ."

GEORGE BOOTH: Edward? I've offered you salvation. *Salvation.*

EDWARD: . . . I thought we were talking about "money."

GEORGE BOOTH: And you spit on me, for my Christian impulses.

EDWARD: How dare you, talk to me about Christian impulses . . .

GEORGE BOOTH: And how dare you. (*To* ALICE) Would you excuse us?

ALICE: I will not.

GEORGE BOOTH: Then I must speak. (*To* COLPUS) Yes?

COLPUS: Edward, I beg you to reconsider Mr. George Booth's offer.

EDWARD: I find it shameful. (*Pause*)

GEORGE BOOTH: Take back the word. Beg my pardon. (*Pause*) Beg my pardon, and I will leave you free.

COLPUS: Consider what he's said, Edward.

EDWARD: I've heard what he's said.

COLPUS: I do not think you have. I have stood here, and heard you speak intemperately to an older man, an upright man, and a friend of your family. Mr. Booth, who has it in his power, has offered, in charity, to leave you free. Now!

EDWARD: I do not believe he spoke in charity.

COLPUS: Then, however you believe he spoke, Edward, I call on *you* to act with charity. Towards Mr. Booth, and towards his motives. To ascribe the higher motive to him, and accept his offer.

EDWARD: His offer is shameful, and cannot be accepted.

GEORGE BOOTH: How dare you, sir, speak to me of shame? (*To* ALICE) Do you know . . .

COLPUS: No, please . . .

GEORGE BOOTH: To the contrary . . . (*To* ALICE) Do you know, do you know why he was leaving his family? Do you know where he was off to? For the holidays?

ALICE: Should I know?

COLPUS: Mr. Booth . . . please.

GEORGE BOOTH: (*To* EDWARD) I ask you one last time.

EDWARD: Do you threaten me?

GEORGE BOOTH: (*To* ALICE) Your upright, worthy lover . . . your, your paragon, your fiancé . . . was off to Europe. To France. To meet a woman. Peacey told me. He arranged it to go with a woman. After . . . after all . . . these years of your connection which is how he's treated you. And how he's treated *all* of us. (*To* EDWARD) And now see how you enjoy having *your* life ruined. You treat us all alike. With contempt. With falsehood, with hatred, hatred. And I don't understand. What have you taken from your father . . . and now to force me to besmirch his name. God damn you. God damn you for what you have done. I swear before God, I'll see you in jail. I'll see you branded as a thief . . .

(HONOR *enters.* GEORGE BOOTH *starts to exit with* COLPUS. COLPUS *exits.* GEORGE BOOTH *lingers to take his leave of* HONOR.)

HONOR: Oh, are you talking business?

EDWARD: We're quite done.

HONOR: I thought, dear Mr. Booth, perhaps you wouldn't mind carrying 'round this basket of things yourself. It's so very damp underfoot that I don't want to send one of the maids out tonight if I can possibly avoid it . . . and if one doesn't get Christmas presents the very first thing on Christmas morning quite half the pleasure in them is lost, don't you think?

GEORGE BOOTH: Yes . . . yes.

HONOR: (*Fishing out the parcels one by one*) This is a bell for Mrs. Williams . . . something she said she wanted so you can ring that for her, which saves the maids. Cap and apron for Mary. Cap and apron for Ellen. Shawl for Davis, when she goes out to the larder. All useful presents. And that's something for you, but you're not to look at it till the morning. (*Pause*)

GEORGE BOOTH: Thank you. Good-bye. (*Pause*)

ALICE: Ethel has left.

EDWARD: Has she?

HONOR: In a rage. Hugh has left. His wife's left separately . . . What a Christmas for departures. And Edward has plans to spend the holidays in France . . . What has become of the family? Why France? Why France at Christmas? All alone . . .

ALICE: No, he was not to be alone.

HONOR: Not alone?

ALICE: No. He was going, we are told, to join a woman.

HONOR: . . . To join a woman . . . oh.

ALICE: (*Pause*) I was to join him there.

HONOR: You.

ALICE: We were to be married. (*Pause*)

HONOR: I . . . Well, then I suppose one may, with propriety, leave you alone together.

ALICE: Yes. I would say.

HONOR: (*Pause*) How odd you are, Edward.

EDWARD: Am I?

HONOR: Quite the most secretive, where do you get it from?

EDWARD: The smash has come.

HONOR: Yes?

EDWARD: It's Mr. Booth. And Colpus.

HONOR: Yes, I see. (*Pause*) I'm sorry.

EDWARD: No, I'm quite happy for it.

HONOR: Why, Edward?

EDWARD: (*Pause*) Because it's right.

HONOR: Does it mean prison?

EDWARD: I believe it does.

HONOR: He gave you no choice?

EDWARD: None. (*Pause*)

HONOR: Poor Ethel.

EDWARD: And not poor you?

HONOR: Oh, nothing will change for me. I've never, actually, had anything.

EDWARD: But the disgrace.

HONOR: Oh, no. I lived through that when father died. Well.

EDWARD: God bless you, love.

HONOR: I don't know what you've done, Edward, but I'm sure you've done the right thing. (*She kisses him.*) Oh, here's the ribbon . . . (*She picks up a spool of yellow ribbon and makes her departure.*) Oh, Alice . . . (*She turns back and kisses* ALICE. *She exits.*)

ALICE: Will it mean prison?

EDWARD: Yes, it will.

ALICE: How long?

EDWARD: Several years. (*Pause*) I won't ask you to wait for me. To marry. No, I . . .

ALICE: Thank you.

EDWARD: Of course.

ALICE: (*Pause*) No, Edward, I couldn't wait for you.

EDWARD: No . . . of course. (*Pause*)

(MAJOR BOOTH VOYSEY *enters.*)

MAJOR BOOTH VOYSEY: What have you done to your family? Edward, I'm speaking to you . . . Alice, will you wait outside?

ALICE: I was just going.

MAJOR BOOTH VOYSEY: Lucky girl, lucky girl, to be shut of him. And what he's done to his family. Edward . . .

ALICE: No, Edward's coming with me.

MAJOR BOOTH VOYSEY: Coming with you? Where?

ALICE: (*Pause*) To France, to be married.

End.

ALSO BY DAVID MAMET

BOSTON MARRIAGE

In this droll comedy of errors set in a Victorian drawing room, Anna and Claire are two bantering, scheming "women of fashion" who live together on the fringes of upper-class society. Anna has just become the mistress of a wealthy man. Claire, meanwhile, is infatuated with a young girl and wants to enlist the jealous Anna's help for an assignation. As the two women exchange barbs, Claire's inamorata arrives and sets off a crisis that puts both women's futures at risk.

Drama/0-375-70665-8

THE CRYPTOGRAM

The Cryptogram is a journey back into childhood and the moment of its vanishing—the moment when the sheltering world is suddenly revealed as a place full of dangers. Set in 1959 and involving an insomniac boy, his anxious mother, and a family friend with a tendency toward deception, David Mamet's play uses events as stepping stones in a series of devastating revelations.

Drama/0-679-74653-6

FAUSTUS

Mamet's Faustus—like Marlowe's and Goethe's before him—is a philosopher whose life's work has been the pursuit of "the secret engine of the world." He is also the distracted father of a small, adoring son. Out of the clash between love and intellect and the fatal operation of Faustus's pride, Mamet fashions a work that is at once caustic and heart-wrenching and whose resplendent language marries metaphysics to con man's patter.

Drama/1-4000-7648-X

THE OLD NEIGHBORHOOD

In these three short plays, a middle-aged Bobby Gould returns to the old neighborhood in a series of encounters with his past that opens windows on his present. Mamet proves himself a writer who can turn the most innocuous phrase into a lit fuse and a family reunion into a perfectly orchestrated firestorm of sympathy, yearning, and rage.

Drama/0-679-74652-8

OLEANNA

A male college instructor and his female student sit down to discuss her grades and in a terrifyingly short time become participants in a modern reprise of the Inquisition. The relationship between the somewhat fatuous teacher and his seemingly hapless pupil turns into an accurate X-ray of the mechanisms of power, censorship, and abuse.

Drama/0-679-74536-X

ROMANCE

It's hay fever season, and in a courtroom a judge is popping antihistamines. He listens to the testimony of a Jewish chiropractor, who's a liar, according to his anti-Semitic defense attorney. The prosecutor, a homosexual, is having a domestic squabble with his lover. And all the while, a Middle East peace conference is taking place. Masterfully wielding the argot of the courtroom, David Mamet creates a world in which shameless fawning, petty prejudices, and sheer caprice hold sway, and the noble apparatus of law and order degenerates into riotous profanity.

Drama/0-307-27518-3

THE SPANISH PRISONER and THE WINSLOW BOY

The Spanish Prisoner, a neo-noir thriller about a research-and-development cog hoodwinked out of his own brilliant discovery, demonstrates Mamet's incomparable use of character in a dizzying tale of twists and mistaken identity. *The Winslow Boy*, Mamet's revisitation of Terence Rattigan's classic 1946 play, tells of a thirteen-year-old boy accused of stealing a five-shilling postal order and the tug-of-war for truth that ensues between his middle-class family and the Royal Navy.

Screenplay/0-375-70664-X

ALSO AVAILABLE:

The Cabin, 0-679-74720-6
Three Uses of the Knife, 0-375-70423-X
True and False, 0-679-77264-2

VINTAGE BOOKS
Available at your local bookstore, or call toll-free to order:
1-800-793-2665 (credit cards only).